## SELMA FRAIBERG

As she so brilliantly demonstrates in her best-selling classic, *The Magic Years,* no one can write more evocatively about childhood and the experience of children than Selma Fraiberg.

Dr. Fraiberg is professor of child psychoanalysis in the Department of Psychiatry at the University of Michigan, and is director of the Child Development Project there. Her most recent book, *Insights from the Blind,* is a remarkable study of development in blind babies.

---

"In teaching us how love is born and how it may die in infancy, Selma Fraiberg has given us a remarkable look at . . . the roots of good and evil in the adult world. She has opened a window to our society's values, and their awesome role in shaping future generations."

—Dr. Julius Segal,
National Institute of Public Health

"If the debate on children and families were to be informed by Selma Fraiberg's fierce and steadfast care for children, the whole next generation would be in her debt."

—Kenneth Keniston,
*The New York Times Book Review*

"Dr. Fraiberg is keenly perceptive, witty, and remarkably readable."

—*Publishers Weekly*

BETTER HOMES AND GARDENS® BABY BOOK
CHILDBIRTH AT HOME by Marion Sousa
COMPLETE BOOK OF BREASTFEEDING
   by Marvin Eiger, M.D. and Sally Olds
EVERY CHILD'S BIRTHRIGHT: IN DEFENSE
   OF MOTHERING by Selma Fraiberg
THE FIRST TWELVE MONTHS OF LIFE
   edited by Frank Caplan
MOVING THROUGH PREGNANCY
   by Elisabeth Bing
NAME YOUR BABY by Laureina Rule
NINE MONTHS READING: A MEDICAL GUIDE
   FOR PREGNANT WOMEN
   by Robert E. Hall, M.D.
PREGNANCY NOTEBOOK by Marcia Colman Morton
PREPARING FOR PARENTHOOD by Dr. Lee Salk
THE ROOTS OF LOVE by Helene Arnstein
SIX PRACTICAL LESSONS FOR AN EASIER
   CHILDBIRTH by Elisabeth Bing
UNDERSTANDING PREGNANCY AND
   CHILDBIRTH by Sheldon H. Cherry, M.D.
YOUR BABY'S SEX: NOW YOU CAN CHOOSE
   by David M. Rorvik with Landrum B. Shettles,
   M.D., Ph.D.

# EVERY CHILD'S BIRTHRIGHT

*In Defense of Mothering*

Selma Fraiberg

**BANTAM BOOKS**
Toronto / New York / London

*This low-priced Bantam Book
has been completely reset in a type face
designed for easy reading, and was printed
from new plates. It contains the complete
text of the original hard-cover edition.*
NOT ONE WORD HAS BEEN OMITTED.

EVERY CHILD'S BIRTHRIGHT

*A Bantam Book / published by arrangement with
Basic Books, Inc., Publishers*

### PRINTING HISTORY
*Basic Books edition published October 1977*

2nd printing .. November 1977    4th printing ...... January 1978
3rd printing ...... January 1978    5th printing ........ March 1978

*Bantam edition / March 1978*

ISBN 0-553-12147-2

*Published simultaneously in the United States and Canada*

PRINTED IN THE UNITED STATES OF AMERICA

*For Jennie, Dora, and Lisa*

# Contents

# V

# VI

# Preface and Acknowledgments

In psychology, as in any branch of knowledge, a time lag may exist between what is known, what is stored in the library, and the uses of that knowledge in the conduct of human affairs. During the past three decades the study of human infancy by developmental psychologists has given us stunning insights into the origins of love and the formation of human bonds. The evidence from diverse studies and schools of psychology converges and has led to this consensus: the human capacity to love and to make enduring partnerships in love is formed in infancy, the embryonic period of development. The child learns to love through his first human partners, his parents. We can look upon this miraculous occurrence as a "gift" of love to the baby. We should also regard it as a right, a birthright for every child.

"Mothering," that old fashioned word, is the nurturing of the human potential of every baby to love, to trust, and to bind himself to human partnerships in a lifetime of love. Under extraordinary circumstances, when a baby has been deprived of a mother or a mother substitute through adversity or disaster or the indifference of his society, we have found that the later capacity of that child to commit himself to love, to partners in love, and to the human community will be diminished or depleted. Unfortunately, the number of such children is growing in our society. In less extraordinary circumstances we are seeing a devaluation of parental nurturing and commitment to babies in our society which may affect the quality and stability of the child's human attachments in ways that cannot yet be predicted.

It is my hope in writing this book to create a bridge—admittedly a narrow bridge—between "what is known" and stored in the library and "what is practiced" in the rearing of infants and in the social institutions which minister to the welfare of infants and young children. This small book cannot do justice to the scientific issues and their implications for children. It can only serve to raise questions and to examine beliefs, attitudes, practices, and policies which affect the development of infants and young children in our society.

The format of this book follows the story as it emerged for me as a researcher and clinician in infant development. Chapters I and II describe those parts of it that came from infant research in human and animal psychology. Chapters III, IV, and V examine the implications of these findings for infants and the social institutions which serve families and their children. The story is a sobering one. The reader may be relieved to know in advance that Chapter VI ends in a spirit of optimism. That's what happens when babies are the subject of a book.

I am indebted to many colleagues who have helped me in the preparation of this manuscript.

For research assistance, I am grateful to John Bennett and Susan Darrow. Joseph and Edna Adelson, Clarice Freud, Harold and Vivian Shapiro read and criticized early drafts and brought their own expert knowledge to me in areas where I cannot claim authority. My thanks to Martha Springer for generous consultation. For fastidious preparation of this manuscript I thank Anita Vander Haagen, Adele Wilson, and Laura Hersey.

My gratitude as always goes to my husband, Louis, who read and criticized several versions of this manuscript. Midge Decter of Basic Books brought wise counsel and her own exceptional editorial gifts to the preparation of the final manuscript.

An earlier version of Chapter II appeared in *Commentary* in 1967 under the title, "The Origins of Human Bonds." Substantial parts of Chapter III appeared in *Redbook Magazine* in February 1975 with the title, "The Right to Know Love." I am grateful to *Commentary* and to *Redbook* for permission to include this material in this volume.

EVERY
CHILD'S
BIRTHRIGHT

# I

## Birthrights

The birthrights which are the subject of this chapter are the rights of infants. They are also the rights of parents. The birth of a child is a celebration of love. Under all favorable circumstances this celebration leads to the conferring of love upon the baby, which is to say that the child is granted full citizenship in the human community. There are ancient traditions which have bound the baby and his parents together from the first hours of life, traditions deeply rooted in our biological heritage. It was not known until our time why the traditions existed or whether in fact the human family should be bound to them. But the evidence that now emerges from a large body of scientific work is incontrovertible: the traditions themselves were "intended" to insure the love bonds between the baby and his parents.

If we now understand the origins and evolution of human bonds, we are indebted for this knowledge to children who were robbed of human partners in their early childhood. The children of war, tyranny, and human disasters who survived without parents or parent substitutes gave their own terrible testimony: the absence of human partners in infancy and early childhood produced a child who had diminished capacity or no capacity for forming human attachments in later childhood or adult life. The best gifts of the psychotherapist could not give these children, who were robbed of their birthrights, that which every baby normally receives in the human family in the first years of life. No one could fill the vacancy within.

Later, in Chapter II, I shall speak of these children. For the problem we are examining in this chapter, it may be enough to say here that it was the "lost children" who had been robbed of their capability for love who caused the scientific community in child development to ask an elementary question: "What goes on between an ordinary baby and his parents that produces a member of the human family who is capable of love that endures?"

Many of the answers have emerged gradually in the past forty years. They are the result of studies which took place during the past two decades. We have identified a language of love, a "dialogue" between the baby and his parents which begins in the first hours of life and becomes elaborated in ordinary experience during the first two years of life. We have decoded the eye language, the smile language, the need language and a large number of signs and signals which had previously gone unremarked and unexamined, because of their "ordinariness."[1]

We have learned how the love bonds are formed, and we have a map for ourselves which shows the development of these bonds in the course of infancy.

And finally, a sobering discovery: we have learned that the human qualities of enduring love and commitment to love are forged during the first two years of life. On this point there is a consensus among scientists from a wide range of disciplines.

We are living in times when there are voices which denigrate the human family and even cry for its dissolution or its recomposition. I cannot identify the voices of infant psychologists among them.

This book is intended for all those radicals, like myself, who think that our survival as a human community may depend as much upon our nurture of love in infancy and childhood as upon the protection of our society from external threats.

In the pages that follow I shall attempt to sketch the story of the development of human attachments in infancy. The story, as it takes form in my mind, wants to follow its own path, one that converges with folk wisdom at many points, touches upon our biological heritage, and brings in some of the central findings in developmental research.

## FOLK WISDOM AND THE REARING OF BABIES

My grandmother, if she were alive, would be astonished to read the reports of infant psychologists in our time.

"Love begins in a mother's arms! Did someone just *discover* this?"

She would be amused by the jargon we have invented to describe the process of mother-infant attachment. "Tactile and kinesthetic stimulation." "Mutual gaze patterns." "Visual stimulus of the mother's face." "Auditory feedback." "Differential stimuli for smiling."

She would be pleased and not surprised to find her own maternal wisdom vindicated by contemporary science.

*The baby can see soon after he's born?* I always knew that.

*The baby smiles to his mother's voice at four weeks?* I told the doctors that myself but they wouldn't believe me.

*The baby recognizes his mother and prefers her before six months of age?* Why not? After all, she's his mother!

*Stranger reactions at twelve months?* Did the doctors just find out?

*A baby should be comforted when he cries?* What mother doesn't know that?

While my grandmother and I would see eye to eye on a number of major issues in infant psychology we would run into problems on rules of evidence. *"If I know,"* her argument would go, "why do I have to prove it?"

We can argue, of course, that my grandmother's folk wisdom has a scientific rationale of its own kind, too. It represents the "findings" of "an experiment" of colossal numbers, the natural experiment of the human race over countless generations. The "experiment" moved with glacial slowness over time; at stake was the survival of the species. The nurturing of an infant was imbedded in traditions which were held sacred in each society. The traditions themselves were derived from biological imperatives. While there were variants in the practices of infant rearing between one branch of the human family and another, one can argue from contemporary studies that all of the branches had more in common in their practices than these differences would suggest.

Watching films of a Philippine tribe, the Tasaday, on TV, I was impressed to see glimpses of infant and child rearing in this "stone-age" tribe which varied only in minor details from "traditional" practices in tribes thousands of miles away, geographically separated by oceans and mountains and economically separated by agricultural and technological attainments which placed them tens of thousands of years apart.

And between the Tasaday practices of infant rearing and those of my grandmother there were not significant differences if we put aside the advances in medical science that my grandmother had available to her.

In my grandmother's time, a baby was delivered at home with a midwife attending and a doctor on call for emergencies. The woman in labor was metaphorically embraced in the arms of her family. Her husband could be there, her mother, women of the family, perhaps—all participants in an ancient rite which united the tribe in a miraculous experience.

The risks to the baby and to the mother were very large even in this era of medicine. I will not argue for home deliveries. But in the ancient tradition the birth of a baby was an exalted experience within the human family. The baby himself was delivered and placed immediately into the waiting arms of his mother. With this embrace, he was initiated into the human community.

Nearly all babies were breast-fed in my grand-mother's time and in her community. They were probably breast-fed for a year or longer. And since the breast and the embrace were one for the baby, he experienced the satisfaction of hunger and the enjoyment of all senses, which we call bliss, in his mother's arms.

Decisions regarding the nutritional needs of the growing baby were largely eliminated for the mother since the self-regulating system of breast-feeding under normal circumstances provided adequacy. Similarly, the inexperienced mother did not need to provide extraordinary sterile conditions for the conduct of the feeding.

During the period of breast-feeding, the mother and the baby were largely bound to each other. Older children in the family could (and did) take over baby care during many hours of the day, but the institution of the hired babysitter was largely unknown. The breast-feeding mother, then as now, could not be separated from her baby for long intervals. This means, of course, that the baby rarely was cared for by a stranger, and was mainly nurtured by his mother.

Neither my grandmother nor any other woman in her generation had a scientific rationale for her infant rearing practices. She could not have told you that all of her traditional practices were "designed" to promote intimacy between an infant and his mother, and that this intimacy led to the unfolding of a biological program which under all favorable conditions established stable and enduring love bonds.

My grandmother would not have been pleased to learn that her infant rearing practices were very close, in principle, to those of a remote village in Mexico, Africa, or India. She was herself literate, respectful of medical science, and vigilant against the microbes that threatened the health of babies. She was also a militant suffragette, but her radical feminism did not alter her methods of infant rearing one iota.

She was, then, a modern up-to-date woman of the first decade of this century, and she would be offended by the comparisons which I find between her practices in infant rearing and those of a "primitive" tribe, as we used to say. She would have found the mothers of such tribes uneducated, superstitious, wanting in hygiene and good housekeeping standards. Any resemblance between their nurture of infants and her own would not have interested her. How else, she would have asked, can you rear a baby given the fact that all babies are constitutionally alike the world over?

Since I do not share my grandmother's prejudices against "primitive tribes" I have allowed my imagination to create an impossible situation in which three contemporary tribes from undeveloped regions are brought together with a modern industrialized tribe for a fruitful exchange on the subject of infant rearing. For this purpose I have invented an International Congress of Mothers and Babies and have recorded the proceedings to advance our discussion.

## Proceedings of the First International Congress of Mothers and Babies

Delegations from four geographically isolated regions are invited to this Congress. Tribe A has its home in a rural region in Mexico. Tribe B has

its origins in Africa. Tribe C occupies a remote village in India. Tribe D lives in a village in North
America.

Mothers with infants under three are encour-
aged to bring them along to the sessions of the
Congress.

## Introductions

At the usual informal get-together that pre-
cedes all such congresses, it is impressive to see
that each tribe has its own style of carrying babies.
Tribe A carries its babies in a shawl, ingeniously
wrapped around the baby so that he is suspended
at breast level. Tribe B mothers suspend the small
baby from a shoulder sling. Tribe C carries its babies snugly wrapped at the breast in a fold of
the mother's garment. Tribe D carries its babies
(a) in the arms of the mother, (b) in a basket
with handles, (c) in a back-pack, (d) in a
wheeled carriage, (e) in a molded plastic seat.

It is immediately apparent that in mode of
infant transport Tribes A, B, and C, though geographically isolated, have more in common with
each other than with Tribe D. The reasons are also
apparent. Since nearly all of the babies in Tribes
A, B, and C are breast-fed, the modes of carrying
the baby were "invented" to bring the baby close
to the source of supply.

During the usual inaugural speeches of a conference, the four tribes outdo each other in prais-
ing infancy and motherhood. But no one can
match the record of Tribe D. In Tribe D the exal-
tation of child and mother is celebrated in sacred
rites. No candidate for public office in this tribe
can be elected unless he kisses at least one baby
in front of a camera. Motherhood is celebrated

once a year on a special day called "Mother's Day." On this day pilgrims line the highways in bumper-to-bumper traffic jams to bring floral offerings and other gifts to mothers.

### Session #1: Infant Health

Spokesmen from each tribe present their latest statistics on infant mortality and infant disease. Charts, graphs, and tables are projected on a screen and the nimble-witted who can read these things can easily see that everyone is lying a little bit. With a statistical correction for tribal vanity, it can be seen that Tribes A, B, and C lag far behind Tribe D in eradicating death and illness in infants, but their death and disease rates are not significantly different from those of impoverished families within Tribe D.[2]

The Conference is off to a bad start. It is not a good idea to bring in statistical charts at the start of a meeting. Some delegates from all four tribes are dozing. Others are kept in an alert state through the tending to complaining babies and the pursuit of restless toddlers.

A glance at the program will tell us that the next topics on the agenda should be of more general interest to the audience.

### Session #2: Tactile and Kinesthetic Stimulation in Infancy

"Tactile and Kinesthetic Stimulation in Infancy" is a lecture given by a distinguished Tribe D psychiatrist.

Much of the doctor's speech cannot be easily rendered in the polylingual simultaneous translation. When it is finally summarized, the mothers of tribes A, B, and C are dumbfounded to hear that

while they have been holding their babies, nursing
their babies, and transporting their babies they
have been giving tactile and kinesthetic stimulation to the baby which is essential for his neuro-
physiological maturation *and* for his emotional
well-being.[3]

"I never realized that!" says a Tribe B mother
to her neighbor. "It just goes to show. Even at a
lousy conference like this you can always come
away with a new idea."

### Session #3: Feeding Your Baby

Feeding your baby brings about lively debate among the delegates. Nearly all the mothers
in Tribes A, B, and C breast-feed their babies.
But there is disagreement among them on the
optimal time for weaning them from the breast.
Tribe B weans its babies around two years of age.
Tribe A regards this as "early weaning," a bar-
barous practice, and ascribes the vigor and longevity of its tribe to weaning between the ages of
three and five. Tribe B argues that when it comes
to vigor and longevity, it can match any other
tribe at the Congress.

The Tribe D delegation applauds breast-feeding "whenever possible." Mainly Tribe D babies
are fed a scientific formula in plastic bottles. The
vigor and longevity of Tribe D is cited in support
of the scientific formula in plastic bottles. A minor-
ity of women in the Tribe D delegation argue the
merits of the plastic bottle for those women who
do not want to be "tied down." It is not good for
some Tribe D mothers to be "tied down." It is not
good for a Tribe D baby to have a mother who is
tied down. A mother who is tied down might be-

come neurotic, and her nerves would affect the baby.

In the polylingual translation, the idiom "tied down" is rendered literally, and the delegations from Tribes A, B, and C listen with grave and sorrowful faces. Evidently in Tribe D a mother who wished to breast feed her baby was bound hand and foot, and it was to escape this brutal and barbaric treatment that some women in Tribe D resorted to plastic bottles.

### Session #4: Education for Parenthood

Education for parenthood is illuminating, and the arguments are sharp. In Tribes A, B, and C little girls and boys become "child nurses" at an early age. This is shown in a movie. Little girls are seen at play with an infant wrapped in a shawl or a sling, snuggled against the chest. Little boys carry baby brothers and sisters in an improvised sling on the chest or on the shoulders, depending upon the age of the infant. All this takes place under the watchful eyes of the mother. At the age of five, most children in these tribes know "the right way to carry babies," "how to soothe the baby," "how to change a diaper," "how to wash the baby." Pictures are flashed on a screen which show a small girl toting a baby nearly as large as herself, a small boy playing tag with his friends, hoisting an infant occasionally to free his arms.

There are shocked murmurs from the Tribe D delegation. Among themselves, the women of Tribe D whisper "exploitation of children," "no time to be a child," "no time to play." The delegation from Tribes A, B, and C, aware of dissenting noises from Tribe D but not knowing why, sum up their education for parenthood with acerbity. Their methods, they argue, are the same methods which their ancestors have employed for centuries. The mothers of Tribes A, B, and C had carried their younger brothers and sisters because it was a privilege. As for the end result of this education one could see for oneself that every boy and girl will have learned how to take care of a baby when the time comes to bring one's own children into the world.

Tribe D now has the floor. This presentation is illustrated with videotape. In Tribe D little girls and boys are prepared for parenthood through play. This is so they will learn that parenthood is fun. Between the ages of three and five a little girl is given a doll which can be fed by means of a tiny bottle filled with water. The doll will eliminate this water through a tiny hole in its bottom, not quite at the right place, but close enough. Some of these dolls have mechanical devices to reproduce the sounds of a crying baby. Still other dolls can speak sentences from the moment the gift wrapping is removed.

The little girl pretends she is a mommy when she feeds Betsy-Wetsy. The little boy is given toy cars and trucks and he can play "going to work."

It is not good for the little girl or boy in Tribe D to take care of baby brothers and sisters. This is because of "sibling rivalry." It can lead to dropping the baby or abandoning him under a lilac bush.

At puberty, or thereabouts, the girl in Tribe D may graduate to the position of "babysitter." (Since there is no word for "babysitter" in the dialects of Tribes A, B, and C, this is rendered literally and there is an outcry from the delegations of these tribes.) It does not surprise the delegates that a little girl who has learned about babies through playing with a doll should now consider it right to sit on a baby, but what mother in her right mind would permit this? The translation is finally straightened out with dialect renditions which give approximate meaning through the term "baby tender." However, this turns out to be inexact, too. A babysitter in Tribe D is not necessarily a baby tender. Mainly she sits. On a chair. Before the TV.

The baby is usually asleep by the time the sitter arrives. This is prudent since, if the baby were awake, he would tax the arts of the sitter, which have been largely practiced on Betsy-Wetsy. On the rare occasions when the baby wakes up, the sitter will have the opportunity to put her early education into practice.

Video: The baby, upon awakening (and expecting his mother), is confronted with a bleary-eyed apparition wearing dental braces. He immediately sets up a howl. This awakens his older sister. She howls, too. The babysitter discovers the baby is wet. No. Worse. She had not counted on this. Betsy-Wetsy wetsies only tap water.

The changing of the diaper occupies 15 minutes. Unlike the docile Betsy, this baby has a built-in bicycle action which thwarts all attempts to position, and to fasten the diaper. He is changed. Is he satisfied? No. The howls reach a higher pitch. He is hungry, the sitter decides. She staggers to the refrigerator and finds a ready-made bottle of formula.

The sitter now feeds the baby. The baby, of course, is made wrong. This is discovered very quickly by the sitter. She positions the baby correctly. If the baby were Betsy-Wetsy. The baby is

held with his head at a declined angle of 30 degrees, to make sure the contents of the bottle will
drain into him. The baby gags, uprights himself,
and gives the sitter hell.

The sitter carefully places the baby on the
couch and goes away to think. On camera we see
the baby thrashing about in a rage. (Watch out,
Missy! Don't leave the baby on the couch! He's
six months old. He'll go over the edge!)

The sitter is thinking. She has learned to do
this in emergencies. (Don't panic. THINK!) She
now remembers where she left the phone number. She calls the baby's mother. The baby's mother arrives in time to snatch the baby before he
goes over the edge.

How, then, will the girl in Tribe D learn to
take care of her own baby when the time comes?
It is explained that the girl will be employed many
times during the next years as a babysitter and she
will practice on other babies. If she does not learn
well, or if the babies are the wrong kind of babies,
there will be time after her own baby comes to
learn everything she will need to know. There
are books for the new mother in Tribe D. There is
the baby doctor who will answer all the mother's
questions, very patiently, very devotedly, on the
telephone. There are the mother's own girl friends
who have just had babies and have the best up-to-
date information on baby care.

"Not the girl's own mother?" asks a Tribe C
delegate in astonishment.

"Alas. The girl's own mother in Tribe D is
ignorant about today's baby. She has only learned
what was right twenty years ago."

"Then does the girl's mother feel ashamed

and saddened because she has no wisdom to give her daughter?"

"No. This is because the mother of the mother's mother also had no wisdom to give her daughter in her time. It is a beautiful tradition in Tribe D that the wisdom of one generation should not obstruct the path of the next generation. When a woman becomes a grandmother, she can now fulfill her deepest longings. She can take courses in creative writing and pottery. She can learn to play tennis. She can go to the Land of the Sun every winter."

### Session #5: Birth. Care of the Newborn, the Mother, and the Father

Babies are born at home in Tribes A, B, and C. A woman from the tribe who is very experienced in midwifery attends the mother in labor and during the postpartum period.

The mother of the woman may be present. The husband may be present. In Tribe B specially honored members of the tribe are invited to the birth.

It is a sacred event for the woman and her family. It is believed that if one can say loving words to the mother and embrace her she will not be afraid of the pain and when the baby comes she will have loving words on her tongue for the baby and will embrace him.

When the baby comes, there are cries of exultation from the mother, and from all the attendants at the birth. The baby is placed in his mother's arms at her breast. It is believed that the baby must be received in his mother's arms as soon as possible so that he will know that he is loved.

The baby in fact stops his crying and relaxes once he is placed within his mother's arms. The baby's eyes are open. The mother gazes into the baby's eyes and the baby gazes into hers. The mother touches the baby, strokes him with her fingers. She has a lovely smile on her face. The baby snuggles at her breast. His face registers contentment.

This is the way childbirth is described in Tribes A, B, and C. In the immediate postpartum period there are some minor differences in care of the newborn and mother. Thus, in Tribes B and C the baby is put to the mother's breast immediately to encourage sucking and lactation. But Tribe A believes that the first milk is toxic to the baby and "throws it away."

Should the placenta be buried after birth or offered to the Temple? Tribe A cites empirical evidence that a properly buried placenta will insure the survival of the baby and protection of the tribe from floods and disasters. Tribe B has it straight from the deity that She will take offense if the placenta is not presented to the Temple with a traditional sacred prayer.

How shall the tribe protect the newborn infant and the mother against the air which harbors malevolent spirits? Tribe C burns incense to dissipate the lingering spirits and recommends its methods to reduce infant disease and mortality rates. Tribes A and B speak sacred words which they will not divulge at this conference and which drive away the malevolent spirits and reduce the infant mortality rates.

But, alas, the infant disease and mortality rates are very high in Tribes A, B, and C. It is believed that this is because some members of these tribes are careless in the exercise of sacred rituals which, when properly performed, have long protected the tribe against malevolent spirits.

How shall the mother's health be conserved in the postpartum period? Tribe A confines mother and baby to a hammock for forty days. The midwife, the grandmother, relatives, and village matrons attend to the mother, the baby, the husband, and older children. It is also a time to advise the mother on infant rearing, to brew herbal restoratives, and to banish any lingering spirits which have invaded the room of birth. Tribes B and C follow similar practices, but the period of confinement lasts from 14 to 28 days.

In Tribe D, women deliver their babies in a special place called the delivery room in a hospital. This is because of the danger of microorganisms which can invade the mother and baby. Since Tribes A, B, and C do not have a word for "microorganisms" in their dialects, the polylingual translators substitute the phrase "malevolent spirits." This creates a sympathetic response. The delegates from Tribes A, B, and C are able to follow the doctor's presentation approximately.

Because of malevolent spirits in the delivery room of most Tribe D hospitals, the mother can only be attended by doctors and nurses who wear masks to prevent the spirits from invading the mother and baby. The woman's husband, and her mother, cannot be present because they harbor malevolent spirits.

As this registers with the delegations from Tribes A, B, and C there are outcries.

*She is with strangers?*

The medical delegate from Tribe D explains that it is better for the woman to be with strangers.

The husband and the mother might cause the woman to become nervous and it would not be good for the woman to be nervous. Also, it would cause the doctors and the nurses to become nervous, and that would not be good.

In the delivery room, the woman in Tribe D is placed on her back on a table, with stirrups for her feet. Her hands are tied down and she is wrapped in sheets. There are cries of sympathy from certain delegations. It is explained that this is to prevent the malevolent spirits from entering the woman. The woman does not object because she knows it is right. For her pain and her nervousness the doctors give her soothing medications and vapors.

After the baby is delivered, the nurse shows the baby to the mother. The mother may look at him but she cannot yet hold him. This is because of the spirits in the delivery room. Also the mother has many medicines and vapors in her and she may not remember that she has just given birth to a baby.

The baby is now taken away to a room with glass walls. The mother is taken away to another room on the same floor. This is good because the mother needs to rest and the baby would be bad for her nerves. It is also good for the baby. He will learn to be self-reliant, which is very important for a Tribe D member. He will learn the lessons of solitude, which are highly prized in Tribe D and celebrated in the words of their sages: "When everybody leaves you, brother, you've always got yourself."

In many hospitals in the land of Tribe D it takes twelve hours for the mother to rest her nerves and for the baby to become self-reliant. Then the nurse brings the baby to the mother. The mother rejoices. She is now allowed to hold the baby and to feed him. The father is now permitted to hold the baby. And he rejoices.

The mother and the baby will remain in the hospital for three days. The baby will be brought to the mother every four hours for a feeding. Some mothers will breast-feed their babies, and some mothers will feed their babies with the plastic bottle. It is very inconvenient for the nurses when the mother wishes to breast-feed her baby. Some mothers decide it is not good to inconvenience the nurses.

The mother has many hours of solitude in the hospital. The baby has many hours of solitude in the room with glass walls. Sometimes the mother cries. This is called the postpartum blues. It is not known why some mothers have the postpartum blues.

A delegate from Tribe B speaks up. In her opinion, she says, the mother is sad in Tribe D because her baby has been taken away from her. The baby does not belong to the mother when he is born. He belongs to the hospital.

There are murmurs of assent from the delegates of Tribes A, B, and C. A mother from Tribe A speaks up. In her opinion, she says, the mother also feels not loved in the hospital. It is not good for a new mother to be among strangers. In Tribe B a new mother has her baby in her arms and the family has loving arms and loving words for the mother to nourish her spirit.

Three days after the Tribe D baby is born, the mother and the baby are allowed to go home. It is a very great moment for the mother and the father. Now they will learn to take care of their baby. Each day the father goes off to work in his car. The mother must now practice feeding the baby, diapering the baby, bathing the baby, and comforting the baby when he cries. She must clean the house and cook the meals and do the laundry.

There are murmurs of protest from the delegates of Tribes A, B, and C. The new mother should rest! Her mother and her aunts and her neighbors should take care of her household.

In Tribe D, it is explained, the new mother does not need to rest. She is very strong. She has had good nourishment throughout her life. She has studied field hockey and tennis in school. She is very self-reliant.

How does the father come to know his baby in Tribe D?

The father in Tribe D has been prepared for fatherhood. When he was a small boy he began to play "going to work" with his little cars. It was not right that a little boy should learn about babies through feeding dolls and, as things turn out, that may be a good thing.

When his wife is in the delivery room, the doctors and nurses give the father a little room to sit in with other men who are about to become fathers. It is necessary to put the fathers away so that they will not make the doctors and the nurses nervous.

The father in his solitude will have much time to think. He is not sure that he has anything to do with the baby that is about to be delivered and must remind himself how babies are made. The father, it is remembered, planted a little seed in the mother. The father's thoughts turn shyly to the act of love which produced this baby and his eyes meet the neutral, competent eyes of nurses who walk briskly down the hall. He feels vaguely ashamed. The fluorescent lights of the waiting room turn the blue plastic furniture into a garish purple. The father puts a coin in the coke machine and wonders what all of this has to do with a night of love.

In the midst of these reveries a nurse appears and calls his name. "A girl! Congratulations!" In the father's mind this is the moment when all the church bells should be ringing and the news should be trumpeted throughout the land. But the stranger who uttered these words seems not surprised; her smile is false and the words are spoken in a flat, cheery voice that is not the voice of angels.

In a little while the nurse appears with a bundle and the father sees a tiny face in the folds of the cloth. He touches the baby shyly. Somehow in the months of waiting he had imagined that in this moment it would be his wife who showed him their baby. They would laugh together and cry together and a circle would close around the three of them. It would be a celebration of love. He feels awkward tenderness for the baby as he peers into her face. He is deeply moved. But he feels—he cannot explain why—he feels as if he were being cheated out of something.

On the morning that he and his wife and their baby are about to leave the hospital he goes to the cashier's office to pay his bill. There is a businesslike exchange over the bill, and the father receives a receipt to be presented to the nursing station which will discharge his baby. He stops at his wife's room. The baby is wrapped in warm blankets. His wife is dressed and ready. The father feels an exultant cry arise in him. He embraces his wife and his baby, and while the roommate looks on—with interest (and the nurse pays no attention)—they dance a little dance together and cry endearments and sing in unison, "She's ours! She's ours!" In this way, the child in Tribe D is twice born.

The delegates from Tribes A, B, C, and D listen to the Tribe D birth story in silence.

A delegate from Tribe D speaks from the floor.

While it is true, says the delegate, that most Tribe D babies are born twice in the manner described, it is important to record in the Congress proceedings that there are experiments under way in Tribe D hospitals in which the baby is born only once.

One experiment is called "rooming in." The mother and the baby go to the same room after delivery and stay together for three days. The baby has a little bassinet next to his mother. The father visits the baby and the mother and can stay for many hours if he likes. However, this experiment is only thirty years old. It is very radical. Only a few hospitals have tried it.

Still another radical experiment is being tried out in certain Tribe D hospitals. The father is permitted to be with his wife during labor and delivery if he wears a mask and behaves himself well. It is, of course, too early to know the results of this experiment.

The delegates from Tribes A, B, and C are astonished to learn that they and their ancestors have been participating in radical experiments, the merits of which have not yet been proved.

At last a young woman rises from her seat in the Tribe D section. She is holding her baby as she stands. She looks competent, sure of herself, and unabashed before this large audience. She looks familiar to the delegates. For a moment, everyone thinks that she is the babysitter of the video story, grown ten years older, with the braces subtracted. But she is not the babysitter, of course. It is only important to realize that she *could* have been the babysitter grown ten years older. She is an experienced mother, all delegates can see. Their practiced eyes observe that she holds her baby with sureness and confidence and that the baby is bright-eyed, alert, inspecting the strangers with caution, and smiling a beautiful smile for his mother.

The young woman speaks in a clear, tempered voice: "There was nothing in my experience as a Tribe D woman that prepared me for motherhood until I became a mother. Yet, I always loved babies and to me and my husband it was a completion of our love for each other.

"I do not think that Tribe D loves its mothers well. A woman like myself who chooses to be a mother is not valued by my tribe. She is often scorned because she has not used her education to improve herself and her tribe. It is thought that anyone can be a mother or a father since this is only an exercise of biological capacity.

"For childbirth, I was exiled in the hospital.

"I do not remember the moment of my child's birth because of the drugs that were given to me. So the celebration which my husband and I had waited for did not come in childbirth, but was postponed.

"I was allowed to see my baby four times a day at feeding time. It was said that I needed to rest my nerves after childbirth. Yet who could judge the state of my nerves better than myself? Hearing a baby cry in the nursery and thinking that it might be my baby was not good for my nerves.

"Finally, after three days my baby and I went home with my husband. After we entered our house, my husband and I embraced each other like two crazy people. We discovered at once that our baby was the most marvelous baby that had ever been born in Tribe D. And he was, you know. Because for some weeks to come my husband and I had to learn how to take care of a baby and he almost never objected to our mistakes."

A speaker from the gallery asks for the floor. He identifies himself as a physician. He would like to begin with a compliment to the previous speaker, he says.

Clearly, he says, his fellow tribeswoman has overstated the case, since she is the mother of a splendid baby who shows no ill signs in spite of his mother's complaints against the hospital delivery and aftercare. And the mother herself, so tender and so competent, may very well serve to justify the very system she deplores.

"She's one of the lucky ones," calls out an anonymous voice from the Tribe D section.

"My dear," says the physician, kindly, to the woman, "medical science has given you a healthy and beautiful child who will live a span of life undreamed of in earlier times. Your great-grandmother had thirteen children and five died at birth or within the first two years. I deplore, as you do, the sterile and cold atmosphere of the modern hospital, but that hospital has given you a live and healthy baby. What else do you want?"

"Everything," says the competent young woman, unabashed. "In my opinion," she says, "a medical science that has brought such progress in the war against the biological enemies of the infant should have the resources—eighty years after the birth of modern psychiatry—to attend to the psychological necessities of a baby and his parents."

This statement brings wild applause from all delegations. The chair declares the meeting adjourned.

A boy's choir, imported by the local chamber of commerce, sings "M is for the million things she gave me." The multilingual translators do not attempt to cope with these verses. Exeunt . . . All.

## THE BIOLOGICAL PROGRAM AND SOCIAL TRADITION

The impossible meeting of delegates from four tribes which we have attended can lead us to these reflections:

Three geographically and socially isolated tribes (A, B, and C) have more in common with each other in their infant rearing practices than they have with Tribe D, which is technologically the most advanced of these tribes. Also, I have suggested, a great-grandmother in Tribe D would find that her infant rearing methods had more in common with Tribes A, B, and C than with those of her descendants in the late '70's.

These similarities suggest the there are ancient, highly conservative traditions in the human family which have governed the practices of infant rearing and that, for certain reasons, Tribe D departed from these traditions during the 2nd to the 7th decades of this century. The reasons, which we can discern in the Congress proceedings, are themselves related to technological advances which Tribe D has had in its possession. There is every reason to believe that if Tribes A, B, and C had had easy access to the same technology they, too, might have produced changes in their infant rearing practices. However, as representatives of the few isolated and traditional societies which we have available to us for comparison, they can teach us a great deal that has been forgotten.

The subject of this discussion is, after all, the origins of human attachment and of human love, and to pursue the question we are obliged to look dispassionately at the biological and social conditions which facilitate human attachments.

The rigidly conserved patterns of infant rearing we have seen in Tribes A, B, and C are, of course, older than the human race. They are very closely related to infant rearing practices among all primates as we can ascertain through studies of animals in nature.

The baby chimpanzee or monkey, for example, is embraced by his mother soon after birth, and for the entire period of infancy he is cradled in his mother's arms in a close ventral clasp. This is the posture for suckling, for contact comfort, for protection, for grooming, for social exchanges, and for transport. The attachment between the baby chimp and his mother is reciprocal. And it is specific. This body intimacy leads the infant to discriminate his mother and to seek proximity to the mother even when his own mobility begins to give him some degree of independence. The mother's attachment to her baby is also specific. The baby is an active partner in attachment; he elicits nurturing and protective behaviors in his mother.[4]

Accidental (or experimental) separations of the baby and his mother lead to panic states in both mother and child. Infant monkeys, during prolonged separations from their mothers, suffer grief and mourning states that cannot be distinguished from those seen in human infants. Pathological behaviors will occur as the infant settles into a stuporous state.[5]

Also, as we all know now, an infant monkey experimentally deprived of a mother of his species, reared as in Harlow's experiment on dummy mothers, will become an aberrant animal. Among the causes isolated in Harlow's experiments are the deprivation of tactile-kinesthetic experience normally given in the ventral cradling by the mother and the psychological deprivation of a mother who is a partner, actively responding to signals from her baby, providing comfort and—to use the awkward phrase of our science—providing stimuli for the activation of sensorimotor systems in the infant.[6]

In short, the biological program which insured the survival of the young also insured mutual attachment between mother and infant. In the evolutionary course of our own species, the matrix of these affectional systems remained the same, with the important difference that the father in the human family became an important figure in his own right in the development of human bonds.

In the social traditions of infant rearing which are conserved in Tribes A, B, and C we can see the biological pattern as structure beneath the social patterns. The biological synchrony of suckling, tactile intimacy, cradling, comforting, sensory arousal, and communication through signs are rigidly conserved through custom in these traditional societies.

It was not necessary for a mother in Tribes A, B, and C to know that each of the components of this intricate pattern was designed to insure the primary human attachments in infancy. If the mother followed tradition (and if tradition was rigidly transmitted from one generation to another), she produced under all normal circumstances a child who showed all the favorable signs of human attachment at two years of age.

If we search for a single word that underscores this discourse on attachment and love, the word "intimacy" is most apposite. We cannot imagine a human attachment in which intimacy between the partners is not a condition. The traditional patterns of birth and nurture of the infant have the virtue of providing the optimal conditions for intimacy. (A woman in labor attended by loved persons; a baby placed in her arms; a baby at the breast; a prolonged period of lying in, in which the baby is at his mother's side; the breast-feeding which unites the baby and his mother for his nourishment and their mutual satisfaction; the prolonged period of breast-feeding, and the transporting of the baby in a close ventral position.)

Now of course, if a social experiment in infant rearing modifies any component of this intricately complex biological system, it will have effects upon contiguous and interlocking systems. If, for example, we isolate a mother and her baby in the postpartum period, which normally provides the optimal conditions for closeness, intimacy, and fulfillment, we are taxing the parents and their baby to find that completion through their own re-

sources after the homecoming. It is a testimonial
to parental love that most parents and most babies
in Tribe D will "make it," but for many parents
those first days or weeks are strained because the
consummatory moment of parenthood was postponed in the hospital.[7]

If the bottle is substituted for the breast, the
biological necessity for the infant to experience
intimacy in a close ventral clasp must be com-
pensated for through the mother's intelligent
knowing or her intuitive understanding that the
baby needs both food and love in her arms. It is
no longer "built in" to the program. The majority of
mothers in Tribe D who employ bottle feeding
approximate the breast-feeding position in their
bottle feeding of the baby. But there are many
mothers today who feed their babies by means of a
propped bottle in his crib, or who present the bottle
to the baby while he reclines in a plastic seat. There
are many solitary babies today who do not know
the sensual delights and comfort of the embrace.
Since it has been amply demonstrated that body
intimacy in the embrace is essential for the psychological and physiological organization of the infant, the baby of an unknowing mother can be
deprived of essential nutriments for his constitution and for the conditions of attachment.

Whereas the breast necessarily, automatically,
binds the baby to a specific person, his mother, the
bottle does not guarantee this union. The mother
who "knows" or "intuits" her baby's need for her as
a central person will prefer to take over most or all
of the feedings herself. The mother who does not
"know" is easily led into the circumstance where
"anyone" can give the baby his bottle. There are
some babies in Tribe D who are fed by "anyone

handy" in a large household or an indifferent day-care center, and these babies do not seem to discriminate their mothers from other persons at an age where most babies show preference for and valuation of the mother.

The bottle gives a mother far more mobility than the breast, which is one of the reasons for its growing popularity during the past fifty years. The breast was "intended" to bind the baby and his mother for the first year or two years of life. If we read the biological program correctly, the period of breast-feeding insured continuity of mothering as part of the program for the formation of human bonds. A baby today experiences many more separations from his mother than the baby in traditional breast-feeding societies. How does this affect the stability of the bonds to mother?

In short, where the biological program evolved to insure intimacy and attachment between the baby and his mother and where the conservative social traditions maintained the program, the practices in infant rearing in Tribe D offer options which may or may not provide the essential nutriments for human attachments. It is now the wisdom of the mother which insures the integrity of human bonds. And since many parents in Tribe D are bereft of the traditional baby wisdom which was once transmitted through grandparents, they are adrift in a sea of conflicting advice from experts, from neighbors, and even from a vocal faction of women in the tribe who decry the "slavery" of motherhood.

# HUMAN ATTACHMENT: PUTTING THE STORY TOGETHER

If the reader finds himself at this point with the sensations of jet lag in this story that leaps from biology to social traditions in infant rearing, from folklore to science and science to folklore, it may be the fault of my exposition, but it is also a fair equivalent of the experience of science itself in unraveling the story of human attachments.

This chapter began with an imaginary dialogue between me and my grandmother in which we touched upon some of the scientific findings which bear upon the development of human bonds in infancy. My grandmother seemed not surprised by a summary of major findings. Most mothers and fathers would consider them unspectacular. When we discuss the "language of love" in infant development nearly every parent can recognize the signs. Yet the scientific work goes far beyond the discovery of what is obvious. The importance of this work lies in "putting the story together," in finding meaning, coherence, and design in the sequence of events.

If we now come back to the "language of love" which we have identified through signs in infancy, we will find extraordinary parallels between the "dialogue" of love between an infant and his first partners and the universal vocabulary of love which we normally celebrate as an experience *de novo* in adult life.

During the first six months, the baby has the rudiments of a love language available to him. There is the language of the embrace, the language of the eyes, the language of the smile, vocal communications of pleasure and distress. It is the essential vocabulary of love before we can speak of love. Eighteen years later, when this baby is full grown and "falls in love" for the first time, he will woo his partner through the language of the eyes, the language of the smile, through the utterance of endearments, and the joy of the embrace. In his declarations of love he will use such phrases as "When I first looked into your eyes," "When you smiled at me," "When I held you in my arms." And naturally, in his exalted state, he will believe that he invented this love song.

The baby's rudimentary love language belongs to an innate repertoire. It is all there, potentially, in the program, but it must be elicited by a partner. (In the rare and tragic cases in which a baby is deprived of mothering he will not gaze into the eyes of a partner, he will not smile, or rarely smile, he will not vocalize, and he will resist the arms of anyone who attempts to hold him.)

The baby who is reared in normal circumstances begins to show preference and valuation for his mother and his father around six months of age, or earlier. We can discern this through the same sign language. He seeks the eyes of his mother, he smiles more frequently for his mother than for strangers, he vocalizes more frequently for his mother than for strangers, he prefers to be held by his mother and will resist the arms of strangers. (All love, even in later life, begins with a feeling of exclusiveness. "You are the one who matters; only you.")

And now between six months and fifteen months the baby begins to show his love in new ways. He complains when he is separated from his mother for a few hours. He's very likely now to pucker up when he sees his mother in her hat and coat, and sitters may report that he cries for a time after she leaves. The baby has discovered that his mother is, for the time being, the most important person in his world. And he behaves the way all of us behave when a loved person is leaving for a journey, or is absent for a while. ("I can't bear to be without you. I am lost. . . . I am not myself without you. . . . You are my world and without you the world is empty.")

If all this seems too extravagant to put into the minds of babies, we need only watch a baby of this age whose mother has been called away on an emergency for several days, or a baby who has been isolated from his mother in a hospital. The face of grief is no different at eight months of age from what it is at thirty years. Loss of appetite, sleeplessness, refusal of comfort from someone else —all this is the same.

From this short sketch we can see that already at the end of the first year, the baby has gone through a sequence of phases in his human attachments: from simple recognition of the mother, to recognition of her as a special person, to the discovery that she is the source of joy, the satisfier of body hungers, the comforter, the protector, the indispensable person of his world. In short, he has learned to love.

For those rare babies who have been deprived of mothers or mother substitutes—babies in institutions, for example—there is no sorrow at the disappearance of a human figure or the absence of another person. Since no one person is valued above others, all people are interchangeable.

Between one and two-and-a-half years of

age, the baby who has formed a deep attachment to his mother is also moving toward some degree of independence and autonomy. His own mobility brings him to explorations of the world around him. He tends to go off on brief excursions around the house or the yard, then return to "touch base" with his mother. She is the safe and comforting center and must continue to be so for some years to come. And now, too, he is an active partner in affectionate exchanges. He will initiate the hugs and kisses with his parents as often as they do.

He can tolerate brief separations at two-and-a-half more easily than he could at one year. But prolonged separations for several days will still create anxiety in him. The anxiety is a measure of his love and a measure of his incapacity, still at two-and-a-half, to grasp fully the notion that a mother, though not present, must be someplace and will certainly return. He can hold on to this notion for a few hours, or a day or two, and then, if his mother does not magically reappear and confirm her substantial existence, he reverts to a more archaic notion: she is lost, he is lost. And he behaves exactly as older people do when the lover has deserted. He cries, he buries his head in the age-old posture of grief, he casts off the advances of well-meaning friends, he cannot rest, and he has no appetite.

From all this we can see that a human infant has within him all the human capabilities for profound and enduring attachments and the full gamut of emotions which we read as signs of love and loss.

The pathways that lead from infant love to the love of maturity can be outlined in this story.

Love of a partner and sensual pleasure experienced with that partner begin in infancy and progress to a culminating experience, "falling in love," the finding of the permanent partner, the achievement of sexual fulfillment.

In every act of love in mature life there is a prologue which originated in the first year of life. There are two people who arouse in each other sensual joy, feelings of longing, and the conviction that they are absolutely indispensable to each other —that life without the other is meaningless. Separation from the other is intolerable. In the wooing phase and in the prelude to the act of love, the mouth is rediscovered as an organ of pleasure and the entire skin surface is suffused with sensual joy. Longing seeks its oldest posture, the embrace.

In the first falling in love, every pair of lovers has the conviction, "Nothing like this has ever happened to me before: I never knew what love could be." And this is true, but only in a certain sense. The discovery of the partner, the one person in the world who is the source of joy and bliss, has its origin in the discovery of the first human partner in infancy. What is new is the *new* partner and the experience of genital arousal with longing for sexual union. Yet the pathway to full genital arousal in mature life was laid down in infancy, long before the genitals could play a dominant role in experience. It was the infant's joy in his own body, the fullness of infant sensuality, that opened the pathways to genital fulfillment in maturity.

Freud said all this seventy years ago, and there were few who believed him.

# II

## The Origins of
## Human Bonds

The bonds that unite human partners are older than man. We neither invented the bond nor own the exclusive rights to it. The enduring ties that join members of a species in couples, in groups, and in complex social organizations exist in many species other than our own.

Stable and permanent partnerships for the propagation of young can be found among some species of fish, and these partnerships endure beyond the period of spawning and raising of the young. Among greylag geese there are elderly couples which have raised their broods and remain demonstrative to each other and solicitous of each other's welfare in an exclusive and cozy domesticity that outlives the biological purpose of the union. Lorenz has described genuine grief reactions among widowed geese. Similar accounts exist of the fidelity of jackdaw couples, even after prolonged separation.

In this chapter I propose to pursue the biological story with particular reference to the work of Konrad Lorenz, and to examine the relationship of love and aggression which Lorenz puts before us in his book, *On Aggression*.[1] The biological story illuminates many problems in human psychology and brings us back to the central issues of human attachment which were posed in Chapter I.

## ON AGGRESSION AND THE BOND

Within the same species that produce permanent bonds among members, *fighting* among members is also a common occurrence. The fighting is regulated by formal rules of conduct and ritual forms of triumph and appeasement. It seems that the "problem" of aggression, which we like to believe was invented by the moral intelligence of man, is no less a "problem" to every species that possesses the bond!

Conflicts between the claims of love and the claims of aggression did not originate with our own intelligent species. The devotion and fidelity of the greylag goose, for instance, is maintained through elaborate rituals which are designed to divert aggression from the partner. Even the device of the scapegoat appears in a simplified form among some species of fish, and is ubiquitous among species that exhibit bond behavior. To put it simply, aggression is channeled *away* from the partner in order to preserve the bond.

The parallels between these phenomena and the data of human development and human behavior are striking. In the course of his development, the child modifies his aggressive urges through love of his human partners. In the case of a child who has been deprived of human partners in the formative years he may lack inhibitions of aggressive impulses or have extraordinary problems in the regulation of his aggression.

In the psychoanalytic view, conflicts between love and hate are central in the human personality. The modification of aggression in the service of love has produced an infinite variety of redirected actions and mental mechanisms which serve to discharge drive tendencies through substitute goals. It has produced in man great love, great work, and the highest moral attainments. And while the same conflicts between love and hate can also produce neurotic symptoms in the human personality, it is well to remember that modification of aggression—through sublimation, for example—can bring successful solutions to these conflicts without resorting to disease.

Naturally, at a time when the most intelligent of animals seems bent on the extermination of his own species, a study of the natural history of aggression and its relationship to the love bonds would prove instructive. This is not to say that the solutions that have evolved among sea animals and birds are applicable to human society. When Lorenz urges us to regard the lessons from biology with modesty, he is not suggesting that we employ the rituals of waterfowl to regulate our daily aggressions or our foreign policy. He is telling us that there is an evolutionary tendency at work which has produced ever more complex and effective means of regulating aggression, that this tendency is at work within human society in ways that we cannot easily recognize without following the biological narrative, and that at this point in our history there are as many portents for solutions to the ancient problems of human aggression as there are portents of disaster.

## THE PARADOX

At the center of Lorenz's book is a paradox. (1) Intraspecific aggression—fighting among the members of the same species—is a characteristic of some species but not of others. (2) *Yet the bond appears only in those species which also manifest intraspecific aggression!* (3) There are species that have intraspecific aggression and no bond, but conversely, there are no species that have the bond and do not also have intraspecific aggression. (4) Within those species which have evolved enduring attachments among members, there are biological mechanisms for inhibiting aggression under certain conditions and there are ritual forms of courtship and greeting ceremonials among members in which the characteristic motor patterns of aggression have undergone a transformation in the service of love.

It appears, then, that there are phylogenetic links between aggression and love. The coexistence of intraspecific aggression and the bond in certain species should inform us of the biological purpose and earliest interdependence of two instinctual drives which have evolved as polar and antagonistic. This is the territory that Lorenz explores.

Among the human psychologies, psychoanalysis maintains its position with regard to the instinctual drives. In 1920, when the earlier libido theory was modified by Freud, aggression was given full status as an instinctual drive; a two-drive theory (sexual and aggressive) has remained central to psychoanalytic theory since that time. While recent advances in psychoanalytic theory have been in the area of ego psychology, psychoanalytic ego psychology has, on the whole, remained firmly rooted in biological foundations. It is the ego's role as a regulator of drives, the ego as the agency of adaptation, the ego as the mediator between drives and the demands of conscience, that define ego for psychoanalysis.

Now, it matters a great deal whether we include drives in our theory or not. If we believe that an aggressive drive is part of the biological inheritance of man, we add another dimension of meaning to conflict. It means that we grant motivational force to aggression that can, at times, be independent of objective circumstances. We thus are able to explain what the behaviorists cannot well explain, the ubiquitous conflicts of love and hate, the admixture of aggression in the most sublime love, the "store" of aggression in human personality which can be triggered by a militant slogan or a boxing match or the buzzing of a mosquito. In this view the aggressive drive is given; it cannot be abolished—although it can be brought into the service of human aspirations by inhibiting those tendencies of the drive that can lead to destructive purpose.

We can learn, then, from the study of biology that the biological "purpose" of aggression is not murder. The killing of a member of one's own species is rarely encountered outside of human society. When it occurs among animals in the wild state, it is accidental. When it occurs in a zoo or an animal laboratory it can be demonstrated that some component in the instinctual organization was deprived of a nutriment which is vital for functioning or of the stimulus for release, and that the intricate network which transmits signals within the instinct groups broke down. In one example given by Lorenz, hens that were surgically deafened for experimental purposes killed their newly hatched chicks by furious pecking. The hen, who does not "know" her young, normally responds to the call notes of the newly hatched chicks, which elicit appropriate maternal behavior. The deafened hens, unable to receive the signals of their young, reacted to the stimulus of the "strange object" and unleashed aggression—heightened in this period by the necessities of brood defense—against the brood itself.

Lorenz defines aggression as "the fighting instinct in beast and man which is directed *against* members of the same species." Intraspecific aggression usually occurs in the service of survival. By warding off competitors within the species, aggression maintains living space and an equitable access to the food supply. Aggression is essential for defense of the brood; in any given species the primary tender of the brood, whether male or female, is endowed with the highest amount of aggressivity. With some rare exceptions, intraspecific fighting is limited to subduing the opponent or causing him to take flight. Lorenz describes ritual expressions of appeasement and submission in the loser of the fight as well as ritual forms of triumph (the "triumph ceremony") in the winner. Lorenz and other ethologists have collected thousands of examples from various species and have analyzed the components of each action in order to determine the specific patterns and variations. Each species, it appears, has its own forms of appeasement and triumph, and the ritual performance becomes a common language in which each gesture, each subtle nuance, has a sign function that is "understood" by every other member of the species. Among wolves and dogs, for example, the submissive gesture is the offering of the vulnerable, arched side of the neck to the aggressor. This is by no means an analogue to a "death wish" in the animal; it is the signal, "I give up," and it derives its function as a signal from the opposite behavior in fighting in which the animal protects the vulnerable region by averting his head. The triumph ritual among dogs is the lateral shaking of the head, the "shaking-to-death" gesture with mouth closed. At the end of this ceremony, the loser retreats and the victor marches off.

This ritualization of innate aggressive patterns is one of the most important links between instinct and the social forms that derive from instinct. The motor patterns for aggression are innate; when another instinct is manifested simultaneously, or when external circumstances alter its aim, the innate motor pattern is still produced but with some slight variation that endows it with another function and another meaning that is "understood" in the common language of the species.

What prevents a fight to the death within a given species? By what means can an animal check the intensity of his aggression before he destroys a member of his own species? There are inhibitions in animals, Lorenz tells us, that are themselves instinctive in their nature. There are inhibitions against killing an animal of one's own species or eating the flesh of a dead animal of the species. Nearly all species have inhibitions against attacking females or the young of the species. These inhibitions are so reliable that Lorenz regards a dog who attacks a female as aberrant and warns the reader against trusting such an animal with children. As we follow Lorenz we see that certain values which for humans are "moral imperatives" have antecedents in the instinctual inhibitions of animals.

Now if we grant that a certain quantity of energy is expended in an aggressive act, an inhibition of aggressive action can leave a quantity of undischarged energy in an animal that does not have a repertoire of behaviors or mental mechanisms for blocking discharge. In this dilemma the most common solution among animals is "redirection," to use the ethological term. That is, the animal switches his goal and discharges aggression on a substitute object. In one of many examples given by Lorenz, a female fish wearing the glorious colors of her "nuptial dress" entices a male. In the cichlid, the colors worn by the female are also the very colors that elicit aggression in the species. The excited male plows toward the female, clearly intent on ramming her. Within a few inches of the female he brakes, swerves, and directs his attack to a hapless bystander, a male member of the species. The foe vanquished, the victorious fish presents himself to his bride in a triumph ceremony, which serves as a prologue to the sexual act.

In this example, the inhibition is provided by the claims of another instinct, the sexual drive, and discharge of aggression is redirected toward another member of the species—an "indifferent object," as we would see it. This is a very simple example of conflict between two drives in a species less complex than our own. The claims of each drive must be satisfied, but the aggressive drive cannot satisfy itself upon the sexual object without obstructing the aim of the sexual drive. Redirection of the aggressive drive toward substitute goals provides the solution.

We can, of course, immediately recognize the behavior of "redirection" as a component of human behavior: in its simplest form it is analogous to "taking it out" on another person or an indifferent object, "displacing" the anger. Among humans the behavior of "redirection" has evolved into complex mental mechanisms in which drives are directed to substitute aims, as in sublimation, in defense mechanisms, and also at times in symptoms. In striking analogy with the drive conflicts of the unintelligent animals, it is the necessity among humans to divert aggression away from the object of love that creates one of the strong motives for the displacement, inhibition, and even repression of aggressive impulses. This means, of course, that the mental mechanisms available to humans not only permit redirection of the drives toward objectives that are far removed from "motor discharge of aggression," but that energy is available for investing the substitute act with meaning far removed from "the fighting instinct." Where aggressive and sexual impulses enter into a work of art, for example, the original impulses undergo a qualitative change and the product in the work itself becomes a metaphor, a symbolic representation of the biological aims.

I do not wish to strain the analogies between "redirection" in animals and in humans. When complex mental acts intervene between a drive and its expression, as in human behavior, we are clearly dealing with another order of phenomenon. It is, for example, the human capacity for symbolic thought that makes it possible for the ego to block discharge of a drive or, more marvelous still, to exclude from consciousness (as in repression) the idea associated with the impulse. In non-human species, where there are no ideas and, properly speaking, no state that corresponds to "consciousness" in humans, there are no equivalents for repression.

Yet, we will find it arresting to see, in Lorenz's animal data, simple forms of symbolic actions, a preliminary sketch for a design that becomes marvelously extended and elaborated in human thought. This is the process called "ritualization" in animals which we have already touched on in connection with the ceremonies of appeasement and triumph in animals. Lorenz presents us with an impressive body of data to show how courtship ceremonies among many species have evolved through the ritualization of aggression.

Any one of the processes that lead to redirection may become ritualized in the course of evolution. In the cichlid we saw earlier how aggression against the female is diverted and discharged against another member of the species in the courtship pattern. Among cranes there is a kind of tribal greeting and appeasement ceremony in which "redirected aggression" is simply pantomimed. The bird performs a *fake* attack on any substitute object, preferably a nearby crane who is not a friend, or even on a harmless goose, or on a piece of wood or stone which he seizes with his beak and throws three or four times into the air. In other words, the ritual redirection of aggression has evolved into a symbolic action.

Among greylag geese and other species, the redirected fighting and its climax are ritually observed in courtship, but they have also been generalized into a greeting ceremonial within the species as a whole. Greylag geese, male or female, greet each other ritually by performing the triumph ceremony. It is the binding ceremony of the group, and the performance of this rite with another member of the group renews and cements the bond, like the handshake or password of a secret society or a tribal ceremonial.

And here we reach the central part of Lorenz's thesis, the evolution of the personal bond. We recall that Lorenz and other ethologists have demonstrated that personal ties among members of a species—"the bond"—appears only among species in which aggression against members of the same species also occurs. Using the greylag goose as a model, Lorenz shows how redirected forms of aggression become ritualized, then follow an evolutionary course to become the binding force among members of the group. Thus, among the greylag geese, a species with strong intraspecific aggression, there are stable and enduring friendships and lifelong fidelity between mates. These are bonds which are relatively independent of survival needs or procreation. Unlike partnerships found in some other species, these bonds are not seasonal or circumstantially determined. The mate, the friend, among greylags is individually recognized and valued; he cannot be exchanged with any other partner. Loss of the friend or mate produces genuine mourning in the bereaved partner. And the ceremonial that binds these birds in pairs and in groups, the ritual greeting, the ritual wooing, the bond of love, is the triumph ceremony which originated in fighting and through redirection and ritualization evolved into a love ceremonial which has the effect of binding partners and groups. Aggression is made over in the service of love.

In the model of the greylag goose, Lorenz traces the pattern of the triumph ceremony in fine detail. The phylogenetic origins of the pattern are probably similar to those described in the cichlid: that is, a conflict between the subject's sexual aims and aggressive aims toward the same object finds a solution in the redirection of aggression toward another, an "indifferent" object. The pattern evolved as a condition for mating and, through ritualization, became part of the courtship ceremonial. In the further evolution of the ritual fight, the triumph ceremony acquired a sign function for the affirmation of love; within the species it became a binding ritual. The ceremony, as Lorenz points out, has become independent of sexual drives and has become a bond which embraces the whole family and whole groups of individuals, in any season.

Lorenz adduces a large number of examples to show the evolution of greeting rituals from the motor patterns of aggression. Among certain birds, the "friendly" confrontation and exchange of signals is barely distinguishable from the threatening stance and gestures of the same species (thus, for example, the expressive movement which accompanies cackling among geese). But close observation and motivational analysis show a detail, such as a half-turn of the head or body, which alters the "meaning" of the motor pattern so that the sign value of the pattern is taken as friendly. The human smile, Lorenz suggests, probably originated in the same way: the baring of the teeth in the primal threatening gesture has been made over into the friendly smile, the uniquely human tribal greeting. No other animal has evolved the act of smiling from the threatening gesture of tooth baring.

Moreover, these greeting patterns, which are found among all species that have personal bonds, are not dependent upon learning. Given certain eliciting stimuli, the baby animal produces the greeting sign as part of his innate inventory of behaviors. If one bends over a newly hatched gosling, says Lorenz, and speaks to it "in an approximate goosey voice," the newborn baby goose utters the greeting sound of its species! Similarly, given certain "eliciting stimuli," the human baby in the first weeks of life produces our tribal greeting sign, the smile.

All of this means that in the process of redirection and the ritualization of aggression in the service of love, a new pattern emerges which acquires full status as an instinct and a high degree of autonomy from the aggressive and sexual instincts from which it derived. Not only are the patterns of love part of an autonomous instinct group, but they have a motive force equal to or greater than that of aggression under a wide range of conditions, and are capable of opposing and checking and redirecting aggression when the aims of aggression conflict with those of love.

While we can speak, then, of innate tendencies that produce characteristic forms of attachment in a particular species, it is very important to stress that these patterns of attachment will not emerge if certain eliciting stimuli are not provided by the environment. In the case of the newborn gosling, the cry of greeting is elicited by the call notes of the species, usually provided by the mother. Lorenz, by producing these sounds experimentally, elicited the greeting sounds from the newborn gosling and actually produced in hand-reared geese a permanent attachment to himself; he became the "mother." In experiments which Lorenz describes in *On Aggression* and elsewhere, he was able to produce nearly all of the character-istics of early attachment behavior in young geese by providing the necessary signals during the critical phase of attachment.

In other experiments in which baby geese were reared in isolation from their species and otherwise deprived of the conditions for attach-ment, an aberrant bird was produced, a solitary creature that seemed unaware of its surroundings, unresponsive to stimuli—a creature, in fact, which avoided stimuli as if they were painful. It is worth mentioning in this context that Harry Harlow in certain experiments with monkeys accidentally produced an aberrant group of animals with some of the same characteristics of stimulus avoidance.[2] In his now famous experiments in which baby monkeys were reared with dummy mothers (a cloth "mother," a wire "mother") the animals be-came attached to the dummy mothers in a striking parody of the species' attachment behavior, but the animals also produced a group of pathological symptoms that were never seen among mother-reared monkeys. They were strangely self-ab-sorbed, made no social contact with other members of the species, would sit in their cages and stare fixedly into space, circle their cages in a repetitive, stereotyped manner, and clasp their heads in their hands or arms and rock for long periods. Some of them chewed and tore at their own flesh until it bled. When these animals reached sexual maturity they were unable to copulate. In the rare circumstance under which a female could be impregnated by a normal male from another colony, the female ignored her young after birth or tried to kill them.

To those of us who are working in the area of human infancy and early development, these studies of attachment behavior in animals and the correlative studies of animals deprived of attachment have had a sobering effect. For there are some striking parallels between them and our own studies of normal development and of certain aberrant patterns in early childhood which I will describe later as "the diseases of nonattachment." In all these studies of animal behavior and human infancy, we feel as if we are about to solve an ancient riddle posed by the polar drives of love and aggression.

## THE DISEASES OF NON-ATTACHMENT

In the earliest years of psychoanalysis, Freud discovered that conflicts between the claims of love and the claims of aggression were central to all personality development. As early as 1905 he demonstrated through the study of a five-year-old boy, "Little Hans," how the animal phobias of early childhood represent a displacement of aggressive and libidinous impulses from the love objects, the parents, to a symbol of dangerous impulses, the animal.[3] The phobia served the function of keeping the dangerous impulses in a state of repression and of preserving the tender feelings toward the parents in a state of relative harmony. This is not to say, of course, that conflicts between drives must lead to neurotic solutions. There are other solutions available in childhood, among them the redirection of hostile impulses in

play and in the imagination. But in all these instances of normal development and even in the
case of childhood neuroses, the motive for the redirection of hostile impulses is love. *It is because
the loved person is valued above all other things
that the child gradually modifies his aggressive
impulses and finds alternative modes of expression
that are sanctioned by love.*

In all this we can see an extraordinary correspondence between the regulation of human
drives and the phylogenetic origins of the love bond
as constructed from the data of comparative ethol-
ogy. Perhaps it might even strike us as banal to
say that human aggression should be modified by
love. We are accustomed to take human bonds as
a biological datum in human infancy. There would
be no point in writing this chapter if it were not
for another story that is emerging from the study
of a large body of data in psychoanalysis, psychiatry, and psychology on the diseases of non-attachment.

The group of disorders that I am here calling
"the diseases of non-attachment" are, strictly
speaking, diseases of the ego, structural weaknesses
or malformations which occur during the formative period of ego development, the first eighteen
months of life. These disorders are not classified as
neuroses. A neurosis, properly speaking, can only
exist where there is ego organization, where there
is an agency that is capable of self-observation,
self-criticism, and the regulation of internal needs
and of the conditions for their expression. In a
neurosis there may be disorders in love relationships, but there is no primary incapacity for human attachments. Similarly, we need to discriminate between the diseases of non-attachment and

psychoses. In a psychosis there may be a breakdown or rupture of human bonds and disorders of thinking which are related to the loss of boundaries between "self" and "not self"—all of which may testify to structural weaknesses in ego organization—but this breakdown does not imply a primary incapacity for human attachments.

The distinguishing characteristic of the diseases of non-attachment is the incapacity of the person to form human bonds. In personal encounter with such an individual there is an almost perceptible feeling of intervening space, of remoteness, of "no connection." The life histories of people with such a disease reveal no single significant human relationship. The narrative of their lives reads like a vagrant journey with chance encounters and transient partnerships. Since no partner is valued, any one partner can be exchanged for any other; in the absence of love, there is no pain in loss. Indeed, the other striking characteristic of such people is their impoverished emotional range. There is no joy, no grief, no guilt, and no remorse. In the absence of human ties, a conscience cannot be formed; even the qualities of self-observation and self-criticism fail to develop. Many of these people strike us as singularly humorless, which may appear to be a trifling addition to this long catalogue of human deficits, but I think it is significant. For smiling and laughter, as Lorenz tells us, are among the tribal signs that unite the members of the human fraternity, and somewhere in the lonely past of these hollow men and women, the sign was not passed on.

Some of these men and women are to be found in institutions for the mentally ill, a good many of them are part of the floating populations of prisons. A very large number of them have settled inconspicuously in the disordered landscape of a slum, or a carnie show, or underworld enterprises where the absence of human connections can afford vocation and specialization. For the women among them, prostitution affords professional scope for the condition of emotional deadness. Many of them marry and produce children, or produce children and do not marry. And because tenderness or even obligatory parental postures were never a part of their experience, they are indifferent to their young, or sometimes "inhumanly cruel," as we say, except that cruelty to the young appears to be a rare occurrence outside of the human race.

A good many of these hollow men remain anonymous in our society. But there are conditions under which they rise from anonymity and confront us with dead, unsmiling faces. The disease of emotional poverty creates its own appetite for powerful sensation. The deadness within becomes the source of an intolerable tension—quite simply, I think, the ultimate terror of not-being, the dissolution of self. The deadness within demands at times powerful psychic jolts in order to affirm existence. Some get their jolts from drugs. Others are driven to perform brutal acts. We can learn from Jean Genet of the sense of exalted existential awareness that climaxes such acts. Victims of such acts of brutality are chosen indiscriminately and anonymously. There is no motive, as such, because the man who has no human connections does not have specific objects for his hatred. When caught for his crimes, he often brings new horror to the case in his confession. There is no remorse, often no self-defense. The dead voice recounts the crime in precise detail. There was no grievance against the victim: "... he was a very nice gentleman. ... I thought so right up to the minute I slit his throat," said one of the killers in Truman Capote's *In Cold Blood.*[4]

Among those who are driven to brutal acts we can sometimes see how aggression and sexuality are fused in a terrible consummatory experience. It is as if the drives themselves are all that can be summoned from the void, and the violent discharge of these urges becomes an affirmation of being, like a scream from the tomb. Yet it would be a mistake to think that such criminals are endowed with stronger sexual urges than others. For the sober clinical truth is that these are men without potency and women without sexual desire, under any of the conditions that normally favor sexual response. These men and women who have never experienced human bonds have a diffuse and impoverished sexuality. When it takes the form of a violent sexual act it is not the sexual component that gives terrible urgency to the act, but the force of aggression; the two drives are fused in the act. When we consider the ways in which, in early childhood, the love bond normally serves the redirection of aggression from the love object, we obtain a clue: the absence of human bonds can promote a morbid alliance between sexual and aggressive drives and a mode of discharge in which a destructive form of aggression becomes the condition under which the sexual drive becomes manifest.

From these descriptions we can see that the diseases of non-attachment give rise to a broad range of disordered personalities. But if I have emphasized the potential for crime and violence in this group, I do not wish to distort the picture. A large number of these men and women distinguish themselves in no other way than their attitude of indifference to life and an absence of human connections.

The hollow man can inform us considerably about the problem we are pursuing, the relations between the formation of human love bonds and the regulation of the aggressive drive. In those instances where we have been able to obtain histories of such patients, it appears that there were never any significant human ties, as far back as memory or earlier records could inform us. Often the early childhood histories told a dreary story of lost and broken connections. A child would be farmed out to relatives, or foster parents, or institutions: the blurred outlines of one family faded into those of another, as the child, already anonymous, shifted beds and families in monotonous succession. The change of address would be factually noted in an agency record. Or it might be a child who had been reared in his own family, a family of "no connections," unwanted, neglected, and sometimes brutally treated. In either case, by the time these children entered school, the teachers, attendance officers, or school social workers would be reporting for the record such problems as "impulsive, uncontrolled behavior," "easily frustrated," "can't get close to him," "doesn't seem to care about anything." Today we see many of these children in Head Start programs. These are the three- and four-year-olds who seem unaware of other people or things, silent, unsmiling, poor ghosts of children who wander through a brightly painted nursery as if it were a cemetery. Count it a victory if, after six months of work with such a child, you can get him to smile in greeting or learn your name.

Once extensive study was begun on the problems of unattached children, some of the missing links in etiology appeared. We now know that if we fail in our work with these children, if we cannot bring them into a human relationship, their future is predictable. They become, of course, the permanently unattached. men and women of the next generation. But beyond this we have made an extraordinary and sobering discovery. An unattached child, even at the age of three or four, cannot easily attach himself even when he is provided with the most favorable conditions for the formation of a human bond. The most expert clinical workers and foster parents can testify that to win such a child, to make him care, to become important to him, to be needed by him, and finally to be loved by him, is the work of months and years. Yet all of this, including the achievement of a binding love for a partner, normally takes place, without psychiatric consultation, in ordinary homes and with ordinary babies, during the first year of life.

This brings us to another part of the story, and to further links with the biological studies of Lorenz. Research into the problems of attachment and non-attachment has begun to move further and further back into early childhood, and finally to the period of infancy. Here too it is pathology that has led the way and informed us more fully of the normal course of attachment behavior in children.

## CLINICAL STUDIES: LOST AND BROKEN ATTACHMENTS IN INFANCY

Since World War II, a very large number of studies have appeared which deal with the absence or rupture of human ties in infancy. There is strong evidence to indicate that either of these two conditions can produce certain disturbances in the later functioning of the child and can impair to varying degrees the capacity of the child to bind himself to human partners later in childhood. A number of these studies were carried out in infant institutions. Others followed children who had spent their infancy and early years in a succession of foster homes. In each of the studies that I shall refer to here, the constitutional adequacy of the baby at birth was established by objective tests. When control groups were employed, as they were in some of the studies, there was careful matching of the original family background. These investigations have been conducted by some of the most distinguished men and women working in child psychoanalysis, child psychiatry, and pediatrics—among them Anna Freud, Dorothy Burlingham, René Spitz, John Bowlby, William Goldfarb, Sally Provence, and Rose Lipton.

The institutional studies have enabled us to follow the development of babies who were reared without any possibility of establishing a human partnership. Typically, even in the best institutions, a baby is cared for by a corps of nurses and aides, and three such corps, working in shifts, have responsibility for large groups of babies in a ward.[5] The foster home studies, on the other hand, together with studies of "separation effects," have enabled us to investigate a group of babies and young children who had known mothering and human partnerships at one or another period of early development and who suffered loss of the mother and often repeated separations from a succession of substitute mothers. In one set of studies, then, the groups of babies had in common the experience of no human partnerships; in the other, the babies had suffered ruptures of human ties in early development.

Within these two large groups the data from all studies confirm each other in these essential facts: children who have been deprived of mothering, and who have formed no personal human bonds during the first two years of life, show permanent impairment of the capacity to make human attachments in later childhood, even when substitute families are provided for them. The degree of impairment is roughly equivalent to the degree of deprivation. Thus, if one constructs a rating scale, with the institution studied by Spitz[6] at the lowest end of the scale and the institution studied by Provence and Lipton[7] at the other end of the scale, measurable differences can be discerned between the two groups of babies in their respective capacities to respond to human stimulation. But even in the "better" institution of the Provence and Lipton study, there is gross retardation in all areas of development when compared with a control group, and permanent effects in the kind and quality of human attachments demonstrated by these children in foster homes in later childhood. In the Spitz studies, the degree of deprivation in a hygienic and totally impersonal environment was so extreme that the babies deteriorated to the mental level of imbeciles at the end of the second year and showed no response to the appearance of a human figure. The motion picture made of these mute, solemn children, lying stuporous in their cribs, is one of the little-known horror films of our time.

As we group the findings on all the follow-up studies it becomes clear that the *age* at which the child suffered deprivation of human ties is closely correlated to certain effects in later personality and the capacity to sustain human ties. For example, in some of the studies, children had suffered maternal deprivation or rupture of human connections at various stages in early childhood. As we sort out the data we see a convergence of signs showing that the period of greatest vulnerability with respect to later development is in the period under two years of life. When, for any reason, a child has spent the whole or a large part of his infancy in an environment that could not provide him with human partners or the conditions for sustained human attachments, the later development of this child demonstrates measurable effects in three areas. First, children thus deprived show varying degrees of impairment in the capacity to attach themselves to substitute parents or, in fact, to any persons. They seem to form their relationships on the basis of need and satisfaction of need (a characteristic of the infant's earliest relationship to the nurturing person). One "need-satisfying person" can substitute for another, quite independently of his personal qualities. Second, there is impairment of intellectual functions during the first eighteen months of life which remains consistent in follow-up testing of these children. Specifically, it is conceptual thinking that remains depressed even when favorable environments are provided for such children in the second and third years of life. Language itself, which was grossly retarded in all the infant studies of these children, improves to some extent under more favorable environmental conditions but remains nevertheless an area of retardation. And third, disorders of impulse control, particularly in the area of aggression, are reported in all follow-up studies of these children.

The significance of these findings goes far beyond the special case of infants reared in institutions or in a succession of foster homes. The institutional studies tell us how a baby develops in an environment that cannot provide a mother, or, in fact, any human partners. But there are many thousands of babies reared in pathological homes, who have, in effect, no mother and no significant human attachments during the first two years of life. A mother who is severely depressed, or psychotic, or an addict, is also, for all practical purposes, a mother who is absent from her baby. A baby who is stored like a package with neighbors and relatives while his mother works may come to know as many indifferent caretakers as a baby in the lowest-grade institution and, at the age of one or two years, can resemble in all significant ways the emotionally deprived babies of such an institution.

## BIOLOGICAL AND SOCIAL FOUNDATIONS OF THE HUMAN BOND

The information available to us from all of these studies indicates that the period of human infancy is the critical period for the establishment of human bonds. From the evidence, it appears that a child who fails to make the vital human connections in infancy will have varying degrees of difficulty in making them in later childhood. In all of this there is an extraordinary correspondence with the findings of ethologists regarding the critical period of attachment in animals.

If I now proceed to construct some parallels, I should also make some cautious discriminations between attachment behavior in human infancy and that in animals. The phenomenon of "imprinting," for example, which Lorenz describes, has no true equivalent in human infancy. When Lorenz hand-rears a gosling, he elicits an attachment from the baby goose by producing the call notes of the mother goose. In effect he produces the code signal that releases an instinctual response. The unlocking of the instinctual code guarantees that the instinct will attach itself to *this* object, the producer of the signal. The registration of certain key characteristics of the object gives its own guarantees that this object and no other can elicit the specific instinctual response. From this point on, the baby gosling accepts Dr. Lorenz as its "mother"; the attachment of the baby animal to Lorenz is selective and permanent. The conditions favoring release of instinctual behavior are governed by a kind of biological timetable. In the case of attachment behavior, there is a critical period in the infancy of the animal that favors imprinting. Following this period the instinct wanes and the possibility of forming a new and permanent attachment ends.

It is not difficult to find analogies to this process in the attachment behavior of the human infant, but the process of forming human bonds is infinitely more complex. The development of attachment behavior in human infancy follows a biological pattern, but we have no true equivalents for "imprinting" because the function of memory in the first eighteen months of a human baby's life is far removed from the simple registrations of stimuli that take place in the baby animal. Yet even the marvelous and uniquely human achievements of cognitive development are dependent upon adequacy in instinctual gratification, for we can demonstrate through a large body of research that where need satisfaction is not adequate there will be impairment in memory and consequently in all the complex functions of human intelligence.

Similarly, there is no single moment in time in which the human infant—unlike the animal baby—makes his attachment to his mother. There is no single act or signal which elicits the permanent bond between infant and mother. Instead, we have an extended period in infancy for the development of attachment behavior and a sequential development that leads to the establishment of human bonds. By the time a baby is eight or nine months old he demonstrates his attachment by producing all of the characteristics that we identify as human love. He shows preference for his moth- and wants repeated demonstrations of her love; he can only be comforted by his mother, he initiates games of affection with her, and he shows anxiety, distress, and even grief if a prolonged separation from her takes place.

I do not wish to give the impression that this process is so complex or hazardous that only extraordinary parents can produce a baby with strong human bonds. It is achieved regularly by ordinary parents with ordinary babies without benefit of psychiatric consultation. It requires no outstanding measures beyond satisfaction of a baby's biological and social needs in the early period of infancy through feeding, play, comfort in distress, and the provision of nutriments for sensory and motor experience—all of which are simply "givens" in a normal home. But above all it requires that there be human partners who become for the baby the embodiment of need satisfaction, social interaction, comfort, and well-being. All of this, too, is normally given in ordinary families, without any reflection on the part of the parents that they are initiating a baby into the human fraternity.

Finally, where the attachment of a baby animal to its mother is guaranteed by interlocking messages and responses on an instinctual basis, we have no such instinctual code to guarantee the attachment of a human infant to his mother. This means, of course, that there are an infinite number of normal variations in patterns of mothering and great diversity in the mode of communication between baby and mother. Any of a vast number of variations in the pattern can be accommodated in the human baby's development and still ensure that a human bond will be achieved. The minimum guarantee for the evolution of the human bond is prolonged intimacy with a nurturing person, a condition that was once biologically insured through breast-feeding. In the case of the bottle-fed baby, the insurance must be provided by the mother herself, who "builds in" the conditions for intimacy and continuity of the mothering experience. As bottle feeding has become common among all social groups in our society, continuity of the nurturing experience becomes more and more dependent upon the personality of the mother and environmental conditions that favor, or fail to favor, intimacy between the baby and his mother.

The bond which is ensured in a moment of time between a baby animal and its mother is, in the case of the human baby, the product of a complex sequential development, a process that evolves during the first eighteen months of life. The instinctual patterns are elicited through the human environment, but they do not take the form of instinctual release phenomena in terms of a code and its unlocking. What we see in the evolution of the human bond is a language between partners, a "dialogue," as Spitz puts it, in which messages from the infant are interpreted by his mother and messages from the mother are taken as signals by the baby. This early dialogue of "need" and "an answer to need," becomes a highly differentiated signal system in the early months of life; it is, properly speaking, the matrix of human language and of the human bond itself.

The dialogue begins with the cry that brings a human partner. Long before the human baby experiences the connections between his cry and the appearance of a human face, and long before he can use the cry as a signal, he must have had the experience in which the cry is "answered." Need and the expressive vocalization of need set up the dialogue between the baby and his human partners. Normally, too, there is a range of expressive signs in a baby's behavior which his mother interprets through her intimacy with him: the empty mouthing—"He's hungry"; fretful sounds—"He's cranky, he's ready for his nap"; a complaining sound—"He wants company"; arms extended—"He wants to be picked up." Sometimes the mother's interpretation may not be the correct one, but she has acted upon the baby's signal in some way, and this is the crucial point. The baby learns that his signals bring his mother and bring satisfaction in a specific or general way.

The institutional baby has no partner who is tuned in to his signals. As Provence and Lipton demonstrate in their institutional study, since there is no one to read the baby's signs there is finally no motive for producing signals. The expressive vocalizations drop out or appear undifferentiated in these babies. And long after they have been moved to homes with foster families, speech development remains impoverished.

The animal baby makes a selective response to his mother in the early hours of life, and distinguishes his mother from other members of the species. The human baby discovers the uniqueness of his mother in a succession of stages throughout the first year. How do we know this? Among other ways, through the study of the smiling response of the human infant. Our tribal greeting sign, the smile, undergoes a marvelous course of differentiation in the first year. Since the smile connotes "recognition," among other things, we may study differential smiling as one of the signs in the evolution of attachment behavior. In this way Peter Wolff of Harvard has found that the human baby in the third and fourth weeks of life will smile selectively in response to his mother's voice.[8] Wolff can demonstrate experimentally that no other voice and no other sounds in the same frequency range will elicit the baby's smile. Wolff's finding should end the controversy over the "gas smile," and mothers who always disagreed with pediatricians on this score are thus vindicated in their wisdom.

At about eight weeks of age, the baby smiles in response to the human face. As René Spitz has demonstrated, the smile is elicited by the configuration of the upper half of the human face.⁹ A mask, representing eyes and forehead, will also elicit the baby's smile at this age. The baby of this age does not yet make a *visual* discrimination among his mother's face, other familiar faces, and strange faces. But between the age of six weeks and eight months the smile of the baby grows more and more selective, and at about eight months of age the baby demonstrates through his smile a clear discrimination of the mother's face from the faces of other familiar persons or the face of a stranger. Presented with a strange face at the close of the first year, the baby will typically become solemn, quizzical, or unfriendly, and may even set up a howl. This means that a form of recognition memory for familiar faces has emerged in the infant. But in order that recognition memory appear, there must be thousands of repetitions in the presentation of certain faces, to produce the indelible tracing of *this* face with *these* characteristics, which can be later discriminated from all other faces with the general characteristic of the human face. This does not mean that a mother or other family members need to be constantly in the baby's perceptual field. It does not mean that, if someone else occasionally takes over the care of the baby, his memory capacity will be impaired. But it does mean that there must be one or more persons who remain central and stable in the early experience of the baby so that the conditions for early memory function be present. And it means, too, that such a central person must be associated with pleasure and need gratification because memory itself becomes selective through the emotional import of experience. By the time a baby is eight to twelve months old, the mother is discriminated

from all other persons, and the baby shows his need
for her and his attachment to her by distress when
she leaves him and by grief reactions when absence
is prolonged beyond his tolerance. At this stage,
when the mother has become the indispensable human partner, we can speak of love, and under all
normal circumstances this love becomes a permanent bond, one that will embrace not only the mother but other human partners and, in a certain sense,
the whole human fraternity.

The baby who is deprived of human partners
can also be measured by his smile, or by the absence of a smile. If the human deprivation is extreme, no smile appears at any stage of infancy. In
the institution studied by Provence and Lipton the
babies smiled at the appearance of a human face,
and while the smile was not joyful or rapturous, it
was a smile. But whereas at a certain age babies
normally discriminate among human faces by producing a *selective* smile, the institutional babies
smiled indifferently at all comers. There was nothing in the last months of the first year or even in
the second year to indicate that these babies discriminated among the various faces that presented
themselves, nothing to indicate that one person
was valued above other persons. There was no re-
action to the disappearance or loss of any one person in this environment. In short, there was no
attachment to any one person. And in this study,
as in others, it was seen that even when families
were found for these children in the second or
third year of life there was a marked incapacity to
bind themselves to any one person.

These were the same babies who showed a
consistent type of mental retardation in follow-up
studies. In the areas of abstract thinking and gen-

eralization these children and, in fact, institutional babies in all studies, demonstrated marked impairment in later childhood. In ways that we are only beginning to understand, this disability in thinking is related to impoverishment in the structures that underlie memory in the first year of life. The diffusion and lack of focus in the early sense-experience of these infants, and the absence of significant human figures which normally register as the first mental traces, produce an unstable substratum for later and more complex mental acts.

The third generalization to be drawn from all these studies has to do with "impulse control," and specifically the control of aggression. From all reports, including those on the model institution directed and studied by Anna Freud and Dorothy Burlingham[10] and the "good" institution investigated by Provence and Lipton, it emerges that such children show marked impulsivity, intolerance of frustration, and rages and tantrums far beyond the age in childhood where one would normally expect such behavior. Over thirty years ago Anna Freud drew the lesson from her institutional study that the problems of aggression in these children were due to the absence of intimate and stable love ties. Under the most favorable circumstances, the group care provided by the institution usually cannot produce durable love bonds in an infant. Everything we have learned since this sobering study by Anna Freud has confirmed her findings twice over.

And this brings us back full circle to Lorenz's study of aggression and the bond. The progressive modification of the aggressive drive takes place under the aegis of the love drives. Where there are no human bonds there is no motive for redirection, for the regulation and control of aggressive urges. The parallel with animal studies is exact.

## A SUMMARY OF THE EVIDENCE

If we read our evidence correctly, the formation of the love bond takes place during human infancy. The later capacity of the ego to regulate the aggressive drive is very largely dependent upon the quality and the durability of these bonds. The absence of human bonds in infancy or the rupture of human bonds in early life can have permanent effects upon the later capacity for human attachments and for the regulation of aggression.

It would be a mistake, of course, to blame all human ills on failure in early nurture. There are other conditions in the course of human development which can affect the capacity to love and the regulation of drives. Yet the implications of maternal deprivation studies are far-reaching and, if properly interpreted, carry their own prescription for the prevention of the diseases of non-attachment. As I see it, the full significance of the research on the diseases of non-attachment may be this: we have isolated a territory in which these diseases originate. These bondless men, women, and children constitute one of the largest aberrant populations in the world today, contributing far beyond their numbers to social disease and disorder. These are the people who are unable to fulfill the most ordinary human obligations in work, in friendship, in marriage, and in child-rearing. The condition of non-attachment leaves a void in that area of personality where conscience should be. Where there are no human attachments there can be no conscience. As a consequence, the hollow men and women contribute very largely to the criminal population. It is this group, too, that produces a particular kind of criminal, whose crimes, whether they be petty or atrocious, are always characterized by indifference. The potential for violence and destructive acts is far greater among these bondless men and women; the absence of human bonds leaves a free "unbound" aggression to pursue its erratic course.

The cure for such diseases is not simple. All of us in clinical work can testify to that. But to a very large extent the diseases of non-attachment can be eradicated at the source, by ensuring stable human partnerships for every baby. If we take the evidence seriously we must look upon a baby deprived of human partners as a baby in deadly peril. This is a baby who is being robbed of his humanity.

# III

---

## "Divide the
## Living Child"

And the king said, Bring me
a sword. And they brought
a sword before the king.
And the king said, Divide
the living child in two, and
give half to the one, and
half to the other.

I KINGS 3:23

A child is claimed by two mothers. The wisdom of
the court is sought by two contestants. In this century, which a blind prophet once called "The Century of the Child," the ancient tale of Solomon
renews itself in the modern court. The rights of
child ownership prevail. The child himself remains
a mute contestant. Few voices are raised to claim
his human rights.

We are all made witness to the horror through
the video screen, the news story, the picture magazine. And we are all made judges. "How would I

choose? Who is worthy to make the awesome judgement?"

Solomon's sword has become a metaphor. But for the child the metaphor is exact. In the psychological sense, a child can be "cut in two" when the law decrees that his love for two people who are mother and father to him must be severed, and that he must be given to strangers whom the law decrees to be his parents.

Those of us who are specialists in child development are making a strong claim upon the modern court. We are asking for nothing less than "the moral rights of infants and children," the right to know love through enduring human partnerships. This means that any violation of that right through custody decisions becomes a matter of gravest concern to us. It must also become a concern shared by every citizen, by all of us who care about children.

## THE MORAL BURDEN

In fairness to the modern judge, his moral burden is a larger one than that of Solomon. For the ancients, the claims of blood and blood ties were compelling: in the mystical sense, blood ties united human partners, and were the essence of the human bond. In our time, we have come to know that a child's love for his parents is not instinctive, is not a heritable trait like the color of hair and eyes; it is very largely a love that is born of love. The child loves because he is loved, and the beloved partners may be his natural parents or his foster parents or his adoptive parents. Nor do "instinct" or "blood ties" guarantee that a natural mother or natural father will love their child and therefore be loved in return. If our laws do not reflect these modern truths we must look for other reasons.

Certainly there cannot be an enlightened judge today who does not share these beliefs regarding the nature of a child's love. But there are other traditions with ancient roots which may govern decisions regarding the welfare of children. For today, as in archaic times, the child is regarded as the property of his natural parents. "Who *owns* the child?" may be the principle that determines many custody decisions. The "fitness of the parent" can be a consideration when such "fitness" is questioned in extreme cases. "The best interests of the child" is generally regarded as the cardinal principle, but court decisions regarding it more commonly reflect the prior claim of natural parents under circumstances in which the "fitness" of the natural parent is undisputed.

While straining under the weight of archaic law, the enlightened judge of today has another moral burden thrust upon him. The new burden derives from the findings of contemporary psychology which have illuminated the origins of human bonds. As we have seen in earlier chapters of this book, the love bonds between a child and his parents are formed during the early months and years of life. Any circumstances which break these bonds or prevent their formation may damage the psychological development of the child and may permanently impair the capacity to love and to form enduring human partnerships in later life. The judge who must make the crucial decisions for binding and unbinding these ties for children has the crushing moral burden of this knowledge as he makes decisions each day which govern the future of children.

In our courts today there are a few enlightened judges who have brought this new knowledge of the nature of human bonds into their decisions. This knowledge, I am sure, does not help them sleep well at night. For if we understand fully the meaning of loss of love to a young child, the burden on the conscience of the court is a terrible one.

In the story that follows, I have examined a large number of custody cases which have been brought to my attention. I am not a lawyer, of course. My only task is to examine the human implications of these custody decisions for the child and his family.

## BABY LENORE

The case of "Baby Lenore"[1] was widely publicized in 1971. Baby Lenore had been surrendered for adoption by her natural mother soon after birth. In the story that follows we should keep in mind that the legal procedures for adoption were strictly followed.

Baby Lenore was placed with the DeMartino family in June 1970 at the age of five weeks. The adoptive family had been thoroughly investigated and their qualifications as parents were exceptionally high. When Lenore was four months old the natural mother commenced a *habeas corpus* action to reclaim her child from the agency. The litigation that followed involved a contest between the adoption agency, which claimed that the mother was bound by her contract, and the natural mother, who claimed that she had a right to her child. The natural mother prevailed and in May 1971, when Lenore was one year old, the New York Court of Appeals affirmed the decision to return the child to her natural mother.

The events of the next year are well known. The DeMartinos took up residence in Florida just before the Court of Appeals decision was handed down and, with Baby Lenore still in their care, carried on the fight with the State of New York, which now judged them to be in contempt.

In the trial proceedings, counsel for the De-Martinos argued that the sole issue for the Florida court was "the best interests of the child." Two distinguished psychiatrists, Dr. Stella Chess and Dr. Andrew Watson, testified as to the possible trauma which removal might precipitate in the thirteen-month-old child. On the basis of medical testimony the court decided that the baby should remain with the DeMartino family.

From the evidence reported I concur with the decision that "the best interests of the child" in the case of Baby Lenore were served by her remaining in her adoptive home. If I now speak on behalf of the "best interests" of Baby Lenore, from the psychological point of view, I do not want to put aside the personal anguish of the natural mother or that of the DeMartinos during this nightmare in the courts. For the natural mother, the original decision to give up her baby for adoption must have been a torment. Yet once the decision has been made, the child's interests must, I believe, be paramount. For the adoptive parents, who loved their baby, the terror that the child would be taken from them can be fairly equated with that of parents whose child is in danger of death or abduction.

If I say, then, that the child's interests are paramount, it is not without feeling for the natural mother. But the psychological grounds for the decision of the Miami court represent the best that we know about child development today.

Baby Lenore, like every baby who has known parental love, had begun to form her permanent attachments to her adoptive parents in the early months of life. The DeMartinos *were* her parents. At six months of life, or earlier, a baby clearly discriminates between the faces and voices of parents and those of strangers. Even his smile and his vocalizations become "special," preferential for these two people who are the center of his universe. Between six months and one year of age this love is already so binding that even temporary separation, for a day or two, will create distress, refusal to eat, difficulties in sleeping, and mood changes in which sadness and apathy become recognizable signs of grief. When the parents come back, the baby behaves in ways that we all can recognize as "when the beloved returns." There is relief, comfort, clinging, and gradually a return to his old self.

In brief, if we try to describe the reactions of a baby who loses his parents and his world, we can only find analogies with our adult experience of loss through death. The analogy is fair. Since a baby has no way of imagining the return of a "lost" beloved person, he experiences this loss as total, even as we adults experience the death of a loved person. And when the "lost" mother is replaced, even by a devoted substitute or foster mother, the baby does not automatically transfer his love to the new mother. Love has its own laws, even in infancy. Once love is given it belongs to the loved partners.

What could have been expected if Baby Lenore had been returned to her natural mother as the New York Courts had ordered? No instinct exists which would have caused the year-old child to recognize the woman who bore her. The natural mother would, with terribly irony, be the foster-mother, and the baby who had lost her beloved parents—the adoptive but actual parents—would find her natural mother a stranger. There would have followed a sequence of events which I and others have seen in clinical work: a long period of distress for the baby, a turning away from the stranger who was her natural mother, hopeless crying, and finally resignation. If the stranger, who is her natural mother, is patient and loving, some measure of the baby's capacity to love will return and be given to the new mother. But the cost to the child in suffering is incalculable and the effects of this traumatic loss may endure for all the years to come.

But how do we know this? Can a baby under one year "remember" this traumatic separation from his original partners? No, he will probably not remember these events as a series of pictures which can be recalled. What is remembered, or preserved, is anxiety, a primitive kind of terror, which returns in waves in later life. Loss and danger of loss of love become recurrent themes or life patterns. What is preserved may be profound moodiness or depression in later life, the somatic memory of the first tragic loss, which returns from the unremembered past even, ironically, at moments of pleasure or success. What is preserved is the violation of trust, of the ordered world of infancy in which love, protection, and continuity of experience are invested in people. The arbitrary fate that broke the first human bonds may damage or shatter that trust, so that when love is given again it may not be freely returned. And finally, what is preserved is likely to be a wound to the embryonic personality in the first year which may have profound effects upon later development. In the early years, personality is essentially "interpersonality," the self evolving in relation to human partners, the binding of that self to those partners through love and reciprocal love. When the bond is broken, the very structure of personality is endangered, and the mending of personality will be an arduous task for the new partners.

The risks are very great. Whenever we disrupt the love bonds of infants and children, we take an action which has grave implications for the future of the child. When the New York Court of Appeals awarded Baby Lenore to her natural mother, the decision was reached out of simple ignorance of a large body of scientific knowledge that now informs us of the meaning of human bonds in the early years. I am also sure that Miss Scarpetta, the natural mother, could not have known that her baby's best interests now lay in the preservation of the ties to her adoptive parents. However terrible the choice may be, the good mother who understands this can only decide in favor of her baby's future.

In the largest number of custody cases which I have examined, the court's decisions have been based upon the proprietary rights of the natural parents without regard for the nature of the child's real attachments. There are cases in which children have been reared by grandparents or other relatives, or by foster parents, who are "mother" and "father" to the child in all ways, while the natural parents are strangers or at best comparatively insignificant figures in the child's life. Upon petition by the natural parents the court may award custody to them (if no evidence of gross unfitness is presented) and the child whose love resides with grandparents or foster parents is "cut in two." He may never be made whole again.

It is not only in the courts that the rights of infants are violated. In hundreds of child-welfare agencies throughout the country, babies and young children live in foster homes or institutions for extended periods, because the natural parent or parents are unable to bring themselves to the decision of formal surrender. During the waiting periods, the baby in a foster home has made his human attachments to the foster parents. When the decision is made in favor of surrender by the natural parents, the baby becomes available for adoption. He may be six months old, a year, or two years, or older, when he is wrenched from the foster parents whom he loves, and placed with adoptive parents who are strangers to him. In a number of cases known to me, the foster parents have applied to become the adoptive parents of the child they have grown to love and have been denied by the social agency because agency policy does not permit foster parents to apply for adoption of a child in their care. Such agency policies are buried in antiquity, and I cannot tell you how they came to be. Neither can I tell you why they persist. But in the light of everything that is known about babies and human attachments, thousands of children throughout our country are removed from foster homes where they have known secure love and are delivered like small packages to adoptive parents who are strangers to them. Even the most loving and devoted adoptive parents will suffer many trials before the baby transfers his love and trust to them.

## "FITNESS OF THE PARENT"

In still another group of cases, the issue of parental "fitness" is paramount in the court's decision to award custody. What constitutes "fitness" of a parent? I would consider, as you would, that physical and emotional brutality toward a child, neglect or abandonment of a child, severe mental pathology in the parent (certain forms of psychosis, drug addiction, criminal behavior), would under all normal circumstances raise questions regarding the "fitness" of a parent. But my practical experience as a consultant to social agencies and my reading of custody cases shows a pattern that is as eccentric as that which governs the earlier group of cases I have described.

The proprietary rights of the parent have prevailed in courts under curcumstances in which children have been beaten, tortured, and sexually assaulted by a parent. There are cases recorded throughout the country in which parents who are criminal psychopaths and child murderers have regained custody of their children after a few months of "treatment" in a mental hospital. The same blind justice has declared parents "unfit" when judged on the basis of I.Q. alone, or on something which a court judged "a bohemian style of life," or marriage to a person of another race.

In two cases which I have reviewed, parental rights were terminated on the basis of a "low I.Q." in one or both parents. In the A. case (Iowa, 1972),[2] no clinical evidence of retardation was produced at any of the hearings. If there was other evidence of parental incapacity, this was not included in the brief court opinion. Is there scientific evidence that a parent's capacity to love and care for a child is related to intelligence? I know of none. If the judgment of incapacity is made, it must be made on the basis of other evidence, in fact, the evidence that normally applies in the judgment of "fitness" of a parent. If consideration is given to the child's "best interests," then the questions to be asked are still the essential ones: Are there strong affectional ties between child and parent? Are the parents employing their capacities (however limited) to provide the reasonable minimal guarantees to a child—that he be loved, valued, protected, educated? A parent with "a low I.Q." may be able to provide the essential nutriments for child development. If he or she cannot provide "an intellectually stimulating environment" it is only fair to say that there are other parents at the other end of the spectrum who can provide the nutriments for intelligence and yet be unable to provide love and protection.

The "moral fitness" of a parent in a number of cases reviewed by me became an issue in custody cases. In the absence of absolute standards of "moral fitness" each judge is free to judge "fitness" according to his own views. Thus, in New York in 1972,[3] a family court judge transferred custody of a seven-year-old girl from her divorced mother to her father on these moral grounds: the mother was known to be "cohabitating [*sic*]" with a man described by the court as "the paramour." The judge also cited "the character of the neighborhood" in which the mother was living. The Lower East Side, said the judge, was not "a safe place for a small female child to play." The father, who had remarried, was living in a suburban garden apartment. No other evidence of superior "fitness" of the father was introduced beyond legal marriage and a garden apartment.

Both the mother and father were professional middle-class people. The practice of "cohabiting" without marriage is not, of course, restricted to any class, but I have observed that among the poor it is rarely a factor which governs custody decisions. I have also observed that the issue of community environment, which presumably affects all children, is rarely introduced into decisions regarding child welfare when the family is poor. If the moral principles enunciated by this judge were given general application in custody and child-welfare cases, a large part of the child population of New York City would become wards of the court.

The relevant questions for the child in this case were not examined in the summary that was available to me. What was the nature of the child's attachment to her mother? To her father? What were the demonstrated capacities of the mother to rear her child? What qualified professional opinions did the judge have available to him in making his decision?

In Alabama, in 1972,[4] welfare authorities brought child custody proceedings against a young white woman, twice divorced, who gave birth to a child fathered by a black man. The state tried to take away this baby and her four other white children on the grounds that the mother was unfit. No evidence of moral unfitness of the mother was introduced beyond the implied "unfitness" of a woman who had borne a child to a black man. The juvenile court ruled that the state could take none of the children.

Consider the alternatives. Had the court removed these five children from their mother's custody, the children would, of course, have been placed in foster homes or institutions. The baby, child of a black father and white mother, would have been among the "difficult to place" babies, in this community as in others, and his tragic story could be predicted from that moment on.

Here the court's wisdom prevailed; but in many other instances known to me a righteous judge, committed to his private moral beliefs, has removed children from their homes, from the only human attachments they have known, and set them on a course which is marked like a refugee trail. The family is split up. The children are placed with licensed foster parents whose good intentions, devotion, and humanity are rewarded by that court with the sum of $80 or $90 a month in many communities. The children, if they have had strong attachments to their own parents, are not grateful to their foster parents. Within a year or less, it is entirely possible that circumstances within the foster home might require that the children be placed in another home. It is not unusual in foster-home agencies that children placed at the age of five will know six or seven foster homes before they have reached the age of 12.[5] These are the children who learn at an early age that they are unwanted, unworthy, shabby cast-offs who come to rest briefly in still another place, until they cease to please or to give satisfaction, and then move on again. In one way or another, these cheated children avenge themselves upon society in later years.

The same blind justice that declares a white mother with a black baby "morally unfit," a mother with a low I.Q. "unfit," or a father with a garden

apartment more fit than a mother with a Lower
East Side apartment is at work in another group of
custody cases, where the manifest unfitness and
brutality of parents does not move the court to take
custody of a child in danger.

The capricious motives which have led some
courts to remove children from parents to whom
they had strong attachments are matched, in these
instances, by an irrational justice which is blind to
gross neglect and brutality on the part of parents
and sustains the rights of these parents to own the
children whom they have abused and will continue
to abuse.

There *are* times when children *must* be removed from their own homes. There are children
whose lives are endangered by criminally psychotic
parents, children who have been beaten, tortured,
starved, sexually assaulted by parents who are,
themselves, beyond cure for their terrible mental
diseases. There are parents who do not even experience feelings of guilt for their sadism, or guilt
for the killing of a child. This is not to say that all
abusive parents are beyond cure; a very large number of them can be helped. But among abusive
parents there are a considerable number whom
no known psychiatric treatment will endow with
the capacity for love or simple human caring, or
moderate the rage to kill which breaks through like
a savage storm that is beyond their control.

In every community in this country there are
documented cases in which a judge has sustained
the parental prerogative, ownership of the child,
when the evidence of torture, brutal assault of a
child, or incest was not only presented to the court
but uncontested. Peter and Judith Decourcy have
collected a number of these documents in their

book, *A Silent Tragedy.*[6] The documents read like
a medieval horror story, made all the more terrible
by the court decision: ". . . returned to parental
custody." "Parents admonished to be exceedingly
careful to prevent further injury to these children."

These, then, are the children whose very survival and human potential is in great danger if
they remain with their parents. Foster home placement will provide protection and, under the best
circumstances, a chance to know love and to be
loved. To remain in their own homes is to be de-
stroyed emotionally—and in many cases it is literally a sentence of death.

## WHO ARE THE DECISION MAKERS?

The decision to maintain or dissolve a child's
relationship with parents or substitute parents to
whom he has attachments, or the decision to dissolve or maintain a child's relationship with parents
who are endangering the life of a child, are made
by a juvenile court judge on the basis of evidence
presented to him. He may be assisted in making
his decisions by the testimony of social workers,
psychologists, psychiatrists. These decisions affect
a child's destiny as surely as a pronouncement from
the gods did in ancient justice.

We are all unworthy, being less than gods.
Those of us with professional training in child development know how unworthy. When we are
brought to make decisions we may call upon our
best knowledge and we will surely tremble in awe
before the task. But decisions regarding custody
are finally in the hands of a juvenile court judge,
with the assistance of a supporting staff. What
qualifies the judge to make these decisions which

affect the destinies of children and their families?

Throughout the country, the holder of this office needs no qualifications beyond his legal training. On the judicial ladder, this office is lowest in prestige, least likely to attract a man or woman of superior qualifications and career interests in children and families. The man who must play god need not be informed about the psychological needs of children and their families and is free to exercise his private beliefs and prejudices regarding the best interests of the child without tormenting doubts.

In the majority of our courts, the supporting staff of social workers and psychologists have neither the specialized professional training nor the vocational commitment to children which qualifies them as advisors to the court. In many of the records I have examined, the professional staff dispenses shabby counsel to the court, in which psychological ignorance and confusion are cloaked in pretentious scientific language. Yet they, too, are the decision makers for tens of thousands of children and their families.

Who shall speak for the child in the courtroom? In 1973, Goldstein, Freud, and Solnit published a book in which this question is examined. In *Beyond the Best Interests of the Child*,[7] the authors address themselves to some of the same problems we have considered here. The child's best interests are paramount, these authors assert throughout. The child must have personal representation by counsel in the court. Counsel for the child "must independently interpret and formulate his client's interests, including the need for a speedy and final determination."

What all of us are seeking is an enlightened

court which affirms the priority of a child's needs and his affectional ties over all other considerations. A humane court endowed with psychological wisdom may invoke the principle "in the best interests of the child" and give it a precise twentieth century meaning—that protection and preservation of a child's love for his human partners is a paramount value in establishing "the best interests of the child."

# IV

## Child Care Industries Incorporated

WANTED: MATURE WOMAN.
CHILD CARE. CHIL-
DREN TWO AND
FIVE. EMPLOYED
MOTHER. LIGHT
HOUSEKEEPING.
LIVE IN. MUST
LOVE CHILDREN.
MORE FOR HOME
THAN WAGES.
CALL AFTER 5:00
P.M.
KENNEY 220-7482

Alas for the Kenneys as they wait for the phone to ring. This devoted nanny will not be found. I believe she was last employed by David and Agnes Copperfield, London, circa 1850, having been the childhood nurse of Mr. Copperfield since the untimely death of his father. For a modest wage this cheerful, red-cheeked woman performed all household duties, consoled and advised the widow, and mothered the orphaned child. This good woman literally burst with maternity. Her hearty embraces, recalled by Copperfield the younger, caused the buttons of her bodice to fly off in all directions.

Name: Clara Peggotty; b. 1780 (?); Yarmouth, Exc. ref. . . . . D. Copperfield, C. Dickens, London.
Current employment status: Unknown.

The plight of the Kenneys is shared by approximately 14 million working mothers in search of substitute mother care in 1974. Of these there are 5 million who have 6.5 million children under the age of six. The Kenneys, with their two pre-school children, belong to this second, rapidly growing group of families who must find child care in a society that has been depleted of "substitute mothers." Licensed day-care centers and family day-care homes cannot cope with the demand. The estimated number of day-care "slots" is 1,000,000.[1] In any case, the question must be raised whether these institutions are actually providing "substitute mother care" for babies and preschool children.

To accommodate the millions of children of employed mothers, an industry has grown up which includes sitters-by-the-hour, sitters-by-the-week, "mother's helpers," "day care in my home," and public and private day-care centers. In the last category some enterprising merchants of child care have set up chains which, like Colonel Sanders and Howard Johnson, claim to dispense uniform service and hospitality at reasonable cost. The industry includes hourly service centers for any domestic emergency. Recently I heard of a place called "Kiddie Park," which I thought, naturally, was a playground for small children. This turned out to be literally "a parking place for kids," i.e., you drive up to park the kiddie and for a fee of 50 cents an hour your baby or toddler can have the services of a smiling lady and the society of eight or ten disgruntled and scrappy customers in training pants. We also have "drop-in centers" for babies and young children which operate on the same principle, the principle of the cash and carry laundry or the deposit box at the bank.

For queasy parents who leave a tearful child in the care of anonymous sitters and care-givers, the industry has a slogan: "THE MINUTE YOU LEFT HE STOPPED CRYING."

As an industry, Child Care Industries Incorporated is in a unique position. Its services and personnel can range from "good" to "deplorable," and the consumer in the age range one month to six years will not write letters to the management regarding the quality of service. (Nor is he in a position to withdraw his patronage.) Since his parents are not really the direct consumers of the services rendered, they are rarely in a position to judge the quality. In other trades this is known as a seller's market. The question for us is, "How fare the children?"

As the consumer's advocate I propose to examine the services of Child Care Industries Incorporated from the point of view of both the direct consumer (the child in care and his needs) and the indirect consumers (his parents and their needs).

## THE CHILD IN CARE

We start with the child. But we cannot speak of "the child" or "the working mother" or "the care-giver." The needs of children are different for each developmental stage, and caregiving or substitute mother care must be judged in relation to the reasonable or optimal requirements for nurture at each of these developmental stages.

If we can generalize at all, we can say that all children at all ages need stability, continuity, and predictability in their human partnerships for the fullest realization of their potentials for love, for trust, for learning and self-worth. The human family, which has been unjustly castigated in recent years, is a durable and rugged institution which was invented for this purpose and while fallible at times, it normally provides the conditions for the fulfillment of these needs. When substitute mother care is considered for a child of any age, the questions which need to be asked are: (1) What are the needs of my child at *this* stage of development? (2) Who can serve as a mother substitute for my child, given these needs?

## Infants and Toddlers

For infants and children under the age of three, the developmental needs make special requirements upon the mother and unique requirements for substitute mother care. These are the years in which the foundations for love and for learning are being laid down. Under all favorable circumstances the baby's primary attachments emerge through the mother's and father's caregiving. As in all partnerships of love, the baby's love flourishes through continuity and stability of these experiences with his partners.

The baby's love, like love at all ages, is more or less exclusive. The baby is not more likely to switch partners and bestow his love upon a stranger—even a beguiling one—than any other member of the human family who values his partner in love. By the time the baby is six months old, love and valuation of his mother take on poignant meaning; even minor separations from her can be distressing. And if extraordinary circumstances such as hospitalization or a prolonged journey take his mother away for several days, even the six-month-old baby will show signs of grief and bereavement, more poignantly felt because at six months the baby does not yet have the elementary concept that a person or object that disappears must be "some place."

Between the ages of six months and three years, children who are strongly attached to their parents will show distress and even panic when they are separated from their parents and left with strangers. Parents who understand these reactions as a sign of love take special pains to see that a sitter employed for the parents' night out, or the mother's afternoon away, will be a person known to the child and trusted by them and their child. Most babies and young children can tolerate these brief, everyday separations if substitute care is carefully worked out and if the child, with even minimum language comprehension, can be told that mommy and daddy are going bye-bye, that Susan (the known sitter) will take care of him, and that mommy and daddy will be back soon. In these ways separation from them need not disturb the child's trust of his parents.

As the direct consumer's advocate I must make a blanket indictment of Kiddie Park, the Drop-in Center, Baby Sitters Unlimited, and all such services of Child Care Industries Incorporated, which provide anonymous sitters for small children. During the years when a child must learn trust and valuation of himself and others, these industries teach values for survival. A child cannot feel valued when he is left in the care of a succession of anonymous sitters. And in the population of under-fives which I know well there are large numbers of toddlers and small children who show excessive anxieties around separation and loss which can be attributed in some measure to experiences in which separation has brought a succession of strangers into the child's life.

In the case of the mother seeking employment, who has a baby or toddler, all these developmental considerations take on larger dimensions. Typically, the mother will be gone for ten hours each day, five days a week. Since babies and toddlers make extraordinary demands upon their own mothers, the requirements for a "substitute mother," in the true sense of the word, are also extraordinary. A mother who is in tune with her child, sensitive to his signs and signals, his unique patterns of personality and his idiosyncrasies, will want no less in a substitute mother. If her own pleasure in her child and her own valuation of his love are large, she will want a mother substitute who finds pleasure in babies and small children and who values a child's love. Such a person would also feel that care of a child is a personal commitment and that if she has earned the affection of a small child she would not capriciously change jobs or desert the child and the family to whom she has bonds of affection.

At this point I can feel my readers rise up in bitter protest: where do you find such a "mother substitute?" And in truth, such mother substitutes are in short supply. But remember, I am the consumer's advocate in this essay. And if we are asking the questions, "What are the needs of the child?" and "What are the needs of the family seeking child care?" and "What constitutes 'substitute mother care'?"—these are not the same questions as "What does the market offer?"

If a mother is considering a group day-care program for her baby or toddler, the same questions need to be asked. If group care in a home or a day-care center is considered, the criteria for "substitute mother" do not change.

Is there, in fact, in the home or nursery under consideration "substitute mother care?" Is the program designed in such a way that one person on the staff is the primary and consistent care-giver for each baby? And is this care-giver the "primary person" for one or two babies, or seven or eight babies, under the age of three? Considering the unique needs of the baby and toddler, can one person provide substitute mother care for numbers of small children even if she is highly qualified? And, assuming there is a primary care-giver for each child under the age of three, is this person one who has the personal qualifications of "substitute mother" which we have identified?

Again, I can feel the reproaches of good and conscientious mothers who have sought day care which meets their own high standards. With great fortune some mothers have found an extraordinary home day-care program in which a devoted woman provides substitute mother care. With luck and perseverance some mothers have found an extraordinary day-care center in which the principles of child care are derived from the psychological needs of babies and small children, programs in which exceptionally qualified teachers or aides provide mother substitute care, highly individualized for each child, consistent and mindful of the needs of the small child for continuity in relationships.

I myself know of only a handful of day-care centers in this country which operate on these principles. I do not know of any state licensing laws which include these principles among their standards. Thus, it is possible under existing state laws to prescribe a ratio of adults to children (one adult to four children) in the age range birth to three years and not require that each group of four children should have one primary person who stands in as "mother substitute." It is entirely possible (and usual) that each baby has four to six rotating staff members who care for him, in which case, of course, no one person stands for "mother substitute."

### Preschool—Three to Six Years

Around the age of three, but sometimes later, most children can tolerate separation from the mother for a half day, morning or afternoon, without distress when a good and stable substitute care plan is provided. In developmental terms, the child at the age of three can transfer some part of the trusting relationship with his parents to a caregiver or a teacher who knows how to earn the trust of children. Advances in cognition also help him in tolerating separation; he knows that a mother who is absent will return, that a mother not-present is "some place," while earlier, in the period under three, this concept was either not available to him, or easily lost under tension.

In the years three to six, a half-day group care program based on good educational principles can facilitate the child's development. In a small group social learning can be advanced. In a good preschool program under the leadership of qualified teachers, a child's potential for learning can be enhanced through introduction to stories, to music, to drawing and painting, and exploration of the natural world.

The capacity for peer relationships and friendships at this age has advanced far beyond the two-year level. But the natural tendency of this age is to seek one or two partners in play. A good preschool program is responsive to this tendency and flexibility promotes the conditions under which sub-groups in the larger group can be formed (and reformed). A classroom situation in which twelve or twenty preschool children are put through a daily regimented schedule of "group activities," or a program in which twelve or twenty children mill around a large room without any social structure, are equally inimical to the developmental needs of small children.

The adult care-giver or teacher remains central to the child's well-being during these years (and long after). (The recommended adult-child ratio for preschool [3- to 5-year-olds] is one to seven or eight children. Far better, some of us think, is a one-to-four ratio in which one primary care-giver or teacher is available to four children as "mother substitute" or "special teacher" even though the child will have ties to other teachers.) In a good group program for preschool children one can see the centrality of the adult, as children in the course of a single hour move from peer group play to the adult, "touching base," returning to an activity or to a private pursuit. In an ideal group-care program an adult is available for conversation, for reading a story, for comforting a distressed child, for enhancing a talent or an interest, and responding to this child's personality and his individual needs. (This is also what a good parent does for his child at home.)

Under the favorable conditions described above, most children can profit from a half day in group care. But there is a consensus among good preschool educators that the benefits of a good preschool program diminish or are even cancelled when the school day is prolonged to six hours or beyond. Most children begin to show the strain of prolonged separation from mother and home after a few hours.

When preschool education is the family's only objective in bringing a child to a preschool program, the half day at nursery school is best adapted to the child's own needs. But when the primary consideration is *substitute care for a working mother employed full time*, the 9- to 10-hour-a-day group program can strain the child's tolerance to its limits.

Under the most favorable circumstances, in "ideal" day-care programs known to me, directors and teachers have been unanimous in their reports. When preschool children are separated from their mothers for 9 to 10 hours there is a point of diminishing returns in the nursery day, and finally a point where no educational benefits accrue to the child. By afternoon, after nap time, restlessness, tearfulness, whininess, or lassitude become epidemic in the group of 3- to 6-year-olds. Even the most expert teachers have difficulty in sustaining the program and restoring harmony. What we see is longing for mother and home. The nice teacher, the "best friends," the lovely toys can no longer substitute.

Once again, as I write this, I can feel the reproaches of mothers who for personal or financial reasons must work full-time. As the "consumer's advocate" I am not unmindful of the needs of women who are employed or are seeking employment. But we are addressing ourselves to questions of children's developmental needs and capacities and are examining issues of substitute mother care and education for preschool children. From these points of view it appears to me and others in the field of early child development that an 8- to 10-hour-day group care program for 3- to 6-year-olds does not serve the educational needs of small children, and the professional staff even under the most favorable circumstances find that they do not serve as "mother substitutes" or "teachers" beyond the half-day tolerance of most preschool children.

Are we asking too much? Has anyone proved that the 9- to 10-hour nursery day, under *optimal* circumstances, is harmful to the child? As far as I know, no one has "proved" this. And certainly we would expect that in the ideal nursery I am using for reference, good teachers will exert themselves to see that no child is harmed. In the case of a child who was showing ill effects they would carefully examine the psychological needs of the child with his parents, which might lead to better solutions or alternatives in care.

But here we are speaking of "ideal" nurseries, providing child care for working mothers.[2] They are rare. The majority, by far, of the preschool full-day nurseries that are known to me do not have expert teachers or professional staffs attuned to the individual needs of each child and his family; the programs themselves are not educational programs; they offer, at best, "custodial care." For mothers who are seeking "mother substitute" care and an educational program, these nurseries fail on every count. We do not need to "prove" that such programs can be damaging to many children. When a child spends 11 to 12 hours of his waking day in the care of indifferent custodians, no parent and no educator can say that the child's development is being promoted or enhanced, and common sense tells us that children are harmed by indifference.

The mother who must work for personal or financial reasons has poor options for her preschool children. If she is looking for substitute mother care in a home or a school she will learn that such care will be hard to find "at any price." If we, as consumer's advocates, will not settle for "anything but the best" for children, we are faced with the sobering fact that in our country we will need over 2,000,000 devoted and dedicated "substitute mothers" with professional qualifications to serve the needs of 6,500,000 children under the age of six whose mothers are employed.

For the poor and the socially disadvantaged families, who are a majority in this particular population, a mother's options are usually so limited that "substitute mother care" and "education" are not even among her choices. Children already disadvantaged by poverty, poor nutrition, health problems, domestic stress and confusion, and the risks of high-delinquency neighborhoods, spend their days "at a neighbor's," or several neighbors or relatives in the course of a week, or in a "center" which more likely than not is a storage place for babies and preschool children which, licensed or unlicensed, may offer nothing more than a hot lunch and distracted and overburdened, untrained care-givers.

## The School-Age Child

Normally, the school age child at the age of six or older can manage the full day school session and separations from home with a fair degree of independence. He also demonstrates in his after-school activities some degree of independence in moving outside the orbit of the home. Most parents will agree that supervision and availability of parents or parent substitutes in the after-school hours remain a vital need for the child.

Most mothers who work full time or part time find that the task of combining work and child care becomes easier in the school years. If a good and stable after-school child-care plan is made, the school age child seems able to manage well in most cases. He may, in fact, take considerable pride in his mother's work and can share responsibilities in the home to ease the after-work domestic chores.

The standards for a mother substitute during the after-school hours remain as we have described them for the early years. Someone who can, in fact, "stand in" for the mother between the hours of 3:30 and 6:00, someone who shares the family's standards of devotion to children and responsibility for children. And here, it appears, the task of finding a mother substitute for the after-school hours is not as formidable as in the infancy and preschool years. This is a two-and-a-half-hour work day for another woman. The number of women available for child care on a part-time basis is considerably larger than the number available for full-time child care. In this labor pool are women whose children are grown and who are interested in part-time work, college students who may find part-time child care a satisfying way of supplementing income, women in the neighborhood who are mothers and can accommodate part-time child-care in their own homes, and so on.

It seems, then, that if a mother is in a position to choose whether or not to work, if financial and professional needs are not pressing, her options for substitute mother care are better in the school years than in the preschool years.

It is the problem of child care in the infant and preschool period that presents the largest obstacles for most mothers who are considering employment or are already employed.

## THREE FICTIONAL FAMILIES

As the consumer's advocate I will invent three fictional families for illustration of the problems which an employed mother faces in seeking child care that meets the high standards I have proposed. The fictional families are composite portraits of many young families I have known in my work. I have endowed the parents with good capacities for love and nurturance of children. Their children are at different developmental stages, infancy, preschool, school age. The family options in two families are limited by income. One family, by contrast, has a high income. All three families are served by the enterprise which I have called Child Care Industries Incorporated. The child care people and care facilities are fictional but are drawn from my visits to various homes and centers throughout the country.*

## The Neustadts

This fictional family is composed of Peg, John, and their six-month-old son, Anthony. John is employed in a food store, earning a net income after taxes and other deductions of $7,000. Peg, who had worked as a clerk-typist before Anthony was born, earned $5,000 after taxes. Peg has taken a leave of absence from her job. Without her earnings the Neustadts are just not making it and are already several hundred dollars in debt. Peg makes plans to return to work.

The Neustadts place an ad in the local newspaper. "Mature woman wanted for child care; warm, reliable, must love children." What they had in mind, I suppose, was a 20th-century Peggotty. A single applicant appears, a Mrs. Rosemary Grimm. She is, in fact, a tough old girl, an unsentimental grandmother who states her terms of employment in flat English. She last earned $100 per week at the Masons, and she will not work for less. She produces a long list of references, for the past five years, and two letters from former employers in which she is commended chiefly for her "reliability." It is she who conducts the interview. She is a non-stop talker who notices the baby only once in this hour. With a sharp glance at Anthony (dressed this July day only in a diaper and a cotton vest), she recalls the infant son of a previous employer who nearly died of pneumonia.

The rattled Neustadts bring the interview to

---

*I have chosen the device of "the composite portrait" to protect the identities of real families and day-care programs known to me.

a close. "Not for us!" they say to each other later.
And John makes a quick calculation. At $5,000 per
year for child care, even with tax deductions for
the working mother, the family would net about
$1,000 through Peg's employment.

The Neustadts wait for the other applicants to
appear. But nobody comes.

So the Neustadts enter the world of the sitter
and the mother's helper.

A friend recalled a darling college girl, named
Betsy, who needed daytime employment and had
late afternoon and evening classes. Betsy loved
babies. Her rate was $1.00 per hour.

Three months later, when Anthony was nine
months old, Betsy found a job as counter girl at an
ice-cream parlor for $1.50 per hour. Her girlfriend,
Penny, who loved babies, came to the Neustadts
and left when Anthony was eleven months old.
Penny was followed by Deedee, and Deedee was
followed by Olivia. Olivia was followed by Joanna
who was, herself, the mother of two preschool children who were cared for by a neighbor. When
Joanna left (she developed migraine headaches)
Anthony was eighteen months old.

Anthony began to cry out in his sleep when he
was ten months old. By fourteen months he wak-
ened several times at night screaming "Mama,"
and clung to his Mama in terror when she picked
him up. Peg was alarmed and spoke to friends
about this. Cindy, the neighborhood expert on
child rearing practices, said it was teething. Peg
was doubtful. So am I.

Since I have invented this family anyway I
will invent a nightmare for Anthony which caused
him to waken in terror. In Anthony's nightmare
he is lost in a department store and he can't find

Mama. There is a revolving door which goes round and round and Betsy and Penny and Deedee and Olivia and Joanna and lots of strange ladies keep spinning around, and somebody reaches out and picks up Anthony, and he is sucked into the revolving door and goes round and round. He screams "Mama," and he wakes up and finds Mama beside his bed. He clings to Mama to make sure she won't get lost again.

The Neustadts made another try. A friend recommended the services of Mrs. Nancy Gordon, a young mother herself, who said that she was never happier than when she had a houseful of children. She provided day-care in her home for eight children and she could always accommodate one more. Her fee was $16 per week. Peg went to visit.

Nancy turned out to be a pleasant, vivacious, unflappable young woman. Her basement recreation room housed eight children, four of whom were under two years of age. Two babies were in bouncing seats, suspended from the ceiling. They bounced steadily with glazed eyes. One six-month-old baby was curled up with a bottle propped beside him. A fifteen-months-old baby, clutching pacifier and diaper, roused herself from stupor when Peg came near and cried "Mama!" in an exultant voice. Nancy was amused. "Aw, c'mon, Missy," she said, "that's not your mama." And she gave her a friendly pat. "She says that to everyone who comes in the door," Nancy explained. Three children (ages probably two to three) were sitting transfixed before a television set, oblivious to the world. One child, a boy of four, was riding a trike and appeared to be very much at home. This child turned out to be Nancy's own son.

Question: Is Nancy providing substitute mother care for these babies and young children? Well, not unless the mothers of these babies follow the practice of leaving them unattended for hours with propped bottles, pacifiers, and bouncing seats. Not unless their toddlers spend the day before a TV screen.

But is Nancy an uncaring woman? Is she cruel? Not at all, it appears. If these children seem dispirited and joyless it is not because their caretaker is malevolent or grossly neglectful. She simply doesn't have a sense of what babies and young children need. She is not personally attached to any of these children. She is the custodian of a baby bank, dispensing necessary services such as diapering, a meal and a snack, kleenex for the tears, rescue from assault by peers, safe storage for the ten hours when mother is at work.

In the end Anthony did not go to Nancy's basement day-care program.

Peg's friend, Karen, thought that the Neustadts should look for a good day-care center with people who could give babies the kind of love they need and would ordinarily get at home. The Neustadts now entered the world of the Day-Care Center.

They learned that there were two kinds of day-care centers. One was called "non-profit" (subsidized by public funds) and the other "proprietary" (i.e., privately owned and operated for profit). The Village Nursery (non-profit) charged a fee of $14.00 per week for each child. The director had a teacher's certificate, and the education of her assistants ranged from high school to two years of college. It was rated "good" by local authorities. The Neutstadts learned that they were not eligible for The Village Nursery. Their combined net income far exceeded the ceiling for eligibility for a subsidized center.

The Merry Mites Day Care Nursery (proprietary) charged a fee of $18.50 per week (average for proprietary centers in the Neustadts' community). John Neustadt began to do some calculations in his head. If the subsidized day-care center charges $14.00 per week and the proprietary day-care center charges $18.50, how does the proprietor make his profit?

I went to the library for the Neustadts (I find myself growing increasingly attached to this family) and pulled together some figures. I found that Mary Keyserling (former director of the Women's Bureau, U.S. Department of Labor) had directed a study for the National Council of Jewish Women in 1971.[3] At that time the estimated cost of "quality day-care" was $40.00 per week per child. This means that the non-profit "good" day-care center, such as The Village Nursery, was subsidized for the difference between its $14.00 per week fee and actual costs of $40.00 per week. Without subsidy, the Merry Mites Day-Care Center was charging $18.50 per week and was making a profit, or it could not stay in business. And how were they managing to make a profit?

We will accompany the Neustadts to the Merry Mites Day-Care Center. Merry Mites is located in an elderly house in a low-rent residential neighborhood. There is a small back yard which is fenced off for a play space.

There are thirty children under the age of six at Merry Mites. In the birth-to-three-year range there are ten babies and toddlers. In the three-through-five-year range there are twenty children.

The director of Merry Mites is Mrs. James

Craven. She is not a teacher, she is a business woman. There is one teacher on the staff of Merry Mites, Jenny Gruber. She has had no training in early childhood education. She earns $6,000 per year, which is considerably under the pay scale for teachers in the local school system, but in the surplus teacher market of 1975 she is not doing badly. Jenny is in charge of the three-through-five-year olds. There is one full-time aide on the staff. Her name is Barbara Martin. She has had 2 years of high school and earns $4,160 per year. She is in charge of the infant and toddler group. This gives Merry Mites a staff ratio of one adult per fifteen children. The national median is somewhere between 1:10 and 1:19. The recommended federal day-care staff-child ratios are: infants 1:3, toddlers 1:4, preschoolers 1:7–1:10.

We visit the infant and toddler nursery with the Neustadts. There are two fair sized rooms, one equipped with cots for napping. The play room is equipped with a television set, some mangy stuffed toys, a few battered plastic trucks, a doll carriage, and masonite "doll-corner" furniture, which has not resisted the revenge of a number of Merry Mites. For the babies there are the ubiquitous bouncing swings, each with a mesmerized occupant, and two playpens in which babies in an alert state can engage in brutal socialization of one another. Four of the six toddlers are stretched out before the television set, eyes blank. Two of the toddlers are in battle over the one fire truck (ladders and one wheel missing) and their screams rise above the shrill cries from the TV screen. A mutiny among three prisoners in the playpen group sends Barbara flying in both directions with a shrill command to the firemen to cease and desist—which they do not—and a sharp reproof to the oldest mutineer, Blue Shirt (one year), for causing the mutiny (which he did not). In the clamor Blue Shirt is removed from the playpen and carried off wailing to the cot room, leaving two mutineers still in good form for another round.

There are better moments. When two of the TV watchers desert the screen, they seek out Barbara and climb into her lap. She embraces them both and speaks gently to them. This brings the two firemen and one more TV member over to Barbara's knees. They clamor to be held too. "I ain't got enough lap for everyone," Barbara says kindly. One fireman comes over to the strangers with a beguiling smile and snuggles against Peg's knees. The second fireman, his face blank, moves across the room where he finds his tattered blanket and a pacifier and curls up on the floor.

Who is to blame for this dreary nursery, with its joyless babies? Is it Barbara, who governs this baby bank with a mixture of rough justice and tenderness? I think not. For who could do a better job of playing mother to ten babies for eight to ten hours per day? It is conceivable that even an All Star day-care team composed of Dr. Spock and the American Mother of the Year could not provide substitute mother care for ten babies under these circumstances.

Later we visit the Merry Mites preschool nursery. Jenny Gruber, we remember, is the teacher in charge. The preschool division is housed in the basement recreation room of this old house. Twenty children between the ages of three and six are milling around as we enter. The equipment and toys are battered and ill-chosen by educational standards. A scratchy record player is booming with a rock record. The sound of unearthly laughter is coming from a TV, where a cartoon animal chase is performed before the glazed eyes of five children. There are two trikes with two solemn boys pedalling around the room. Six children are grouped around a table with Jenny, all with crayons and coloring books. The shabby "doll corner" is occupied by three small girls who at this moment are engaged in a shrill fight for possession of one ill-used doll carriage. "It's Joy's turn, girls," says Jenny in a mechanical voice from the table. No one is listening, and the fight continues until Joy wrestles the empty carriage from her competitors and sets out victoriously, wheeling it across the room.

One small fellow attracts our attention. He is the only member of the group who is engaged in what teachers call "creative play." He is at work in a corner of the room with a set of large cardboard construction blocks. He is quite alone, oblivious to the clamor around him. He is methodically building two walls to enclose the corner. There are just enough blocks to bring the height of the walls to the height of a small boy. He leaves an opening at the southeast corner. He crawls in. Over the wall we see him sitting cross-legged on the floor. He has a smile on his face, and it is the first smile we have seen in this joyless throng of children. It strikes me that this lad who has carved out an island of privacy for himself, through his own creative efforts, has exhibited a capacity for adaptation under extreme stress which will insure his survival.

But not for long. Joy and her doll carriage have found him. She pushes her doll carriage through the door of the block house and announces herself. "Stay out!" the hermit screams. There is a tussle in the block house and the walls collapse. The hermit, still cross-legged on the floor, has a monumental tantrum. He is carried from the wreckage, screaming and kicking in Jenny's arms. "You just have to learn to share," Jenny broadcasts above the din. She exiles him.

It is ten o'clock in the morning and Jenny's face looks pinched and hard. Shall we fault her for this mockery of preschool education? I would not. Nothing in her formal teacher education has prepared her for the education of preschool children. Nothing has been added to her education since she took this job. Moreover, even a well-trained preschool teacher could not bring a respectable educational program to this group of twenty assorted kids, ages three to six. One fully trained teacher for four to six children is considered a desirable ratio for a preschool education program.

What Merry Mites is offering the infants and preschool children in the two programs we have visited is "custodial care." Moreover, since Merry Mites has one licensed teacher, good sanitation, and adequate lunches, its rating on Keyserling's scale would be "fair," meaning "largely custodial . . . meeting basic physical needs." About 36 percent of the proprietary centers in the Keyserling study were rated "fair." About 50 percent were rated "poor," among them some which were found to be actually injurious. Only 1 percent of the proprietary centers visited were rated "superior"; 14 percent were rated "good."

Merry Mites "custodial care" for infants and preschoolers begins to look high-grade when we compare it with some of the proprietary centers rated "poor" in Keyserling's study. One excerpt from the report on a day-care center:

> "Very poor basement, dark room. All ages together. Rigid control and discipline. Babies are kept next door in double decker cardboard cribs in a small room with a gas heater. . . ."

Another report, another center:

> "At the time of the survey visit to the center there were two children aged 10 and 12 in charge. This center should be closed. Absolutely filthy. Toilets not flushed, and smelly. Broken equipment and doors. Broken windows on lower level. . . . Broken chairs and tables. No indoor play equipment. One paper towel used to wipe the faces and hands of children. Kitchen very, very dirty."[4]

Then will the Neustadts have to settle for "custodial care," grade "fair," for Anthony? But the Neustadts, we remember, were not seeking "custodial care." They had set out to find "substitute mother care" for Anthony. If the Neustadts were eligible for a subsidized day-care center, would Anthony get "quality day-care?" In the Keyserling study of non-profit day-care centers, only 37 percent were rated "good" or "superior," 50 percent were rated "fair," and 11 percent were rated "poor." This was a better score than the proprietary centers earned in the same study, but no guarantee of "quality."

And if the Neustadts found one of the non-profit centers rated "superior" (9 percent), and if Anthony, competing for its space, could be enrolled, would Anthony get "substitute mother care?" The rating does not guarantee "substitute mother care."

The options for the Neustadts are not good.

### The Andersons

If the Neustadts were a more affluent family, would they fare better in their search for "substitute mother care?" Probably not. The employed mother in a metropolitan community who earns $20,000 or more per year, and who can pay the going rate of $5,000 to $7,500 per year, will find herself in grim competition with her sisters for the vanishing nursemaid. No Peggottys. Not even a latter-day Mary Poppins will appear, although the legend persists. If one is found, lured with TV and private bath, a handsome wage and all fringe benefits, her maternal qualities may not be larger than those of the Neustadts' Mrs. Grimm. But faithful to the legend and the script, this latter-day Mary Poppins will soon rise on her umbrella and leave the nursery vacant once again. The small children of many affluent professional or business women may come to know a procession of indifferent caretakers who come and go. They are interchangeable parts of the child-care industry.

The Andersons are an affluent young couple in their late twenties. Christy, their daughter, is twenty months old. Helen Anderson is a social worker and her husband, Carl, is a lawyer. Helen's salary is $15,000 per year, Carl's income is approximately $25,000. The Andersons live in a suburb of New York City.

When Helen made plans to return to work, Christy was six months old. Helen and Carl had carefully considered plans for Christy's care. They wanted, of course, a nursemaid who was mature, dedicated to children, knowledgeable about babies —a person who would be, properly speaking, "a mother substitute" during the hours when Helen was at work. They were prepared to pay the highest salary without reservations. Helen's own income was not essential to maintain a good standard of living. She chose to work because she loved her work.

The Andersons then set out to find a worthy and capable woman who met their own high standards for "a mother substitute." They registered with employment agencies, placed ads in the newspapers, asked for the help of their friends. The first surprise was the discovery that "at any price," even $7,500 per year, the number of applicants for this special job was pitifully few. Two applicants turned up during the first week of interviewing. Both were women who had unstable employment records and were singularly lacking in the personal qualities that the Andersons were seeking. The trickle of applicants continued for some weeks. . . . A tired grandmother who had reared her own four children and six grandchildren, whose only employment references were in restaurant work. . . . A frayed member of a religious cult whose sentences rambled. . . . A lady who smelled of gin. . . . A cheery girl from a Caribbean Island who spoke little English. . . . An illiterate woman who wrote her name in a labored childlike scrawl. . . .

"At any price" these were all women who had no choice but domestic work. They represented the rock bottom of the woman's labor market, unskilled, uneducated, and without hope in a competitive market.

There were others. Women who were themselves mothers, with their children in the care of grandmothers, aunts, neighbors, desperately seeking work because they were the only source of support for their families. And Helen, who understood these things very well, considered the irony which brought these women to become substitute mothers to the children of other women.

Yet, it was just such a woman, Gladys Harrison, who finally met the high personal qualifications of the Andersons. Gladys was thirty, the mother of three children ranging in age from four to seven. Her two younger children were cared for in a neighborhood day-care center. The oldest boy went to a neighbor after school. Gladys was a personable and intelligent woman. She was charmed by the Andersons' baby and showed beautiful tact in making friends with Christy. She liked the Andersons, and they liked her.

Helen went back to work after Gladys had been with the family for a month of trial employment. There was no question that Christy missed her mother during the day, but there was no question either that Gladys was an adequate "mother substitute." Gladys was always reliably on time early in the morning; she was greeted warmly by Christy, and Christy showed only a few days of transient distress when Helen returned to work. It was a good and a comfortable arrangement.

When Christy was twelve months old, Gladys left the Andersons. Her youngest boy was sick; her oldest boy was having trouble in school; her children needed her at home. She was very sad to leave Christy and the Andersons.

Helen stayed home from work during the next two weeks and began the melancholy interviews again. The second round was not better than the first. And, in fact, one old timer was sent back by central casting for a repeat interview. It was the tired grandmother. In the second interview Mrs. Johnson, the grandmother, seemed to gain in personal qualities and energy. She had the virtue of having no young children at home and her restaurant credentials praised her reliability. After a trial of a week the Andersons decided that Mrs. Johnson had her merits. Her maternal capacities were not as large as those of Gladys. She was competent with Christy, and kind, but the years of rearing too many children and grandchildren had left her without zest for babies. Christy cried now when Helen left. Well, Christy was older, too, and separation from her mother was harder. When Helen called home during the day the sounds of the TV drowned out all conversation and Helen realized uneasily that during Christy's waking and sleeping hours Mrs. Johnson spent a very large amount of time watching soap operas. So did Christy. Christy was whiny and clinging now. Was it the age? Or missing her mother? Certainly as soon as Helen and Carl arrived home from work Christy began a whiny complaint and required a lot of holding and comforting.

When Christy was fourteen months old Mrs. Johnson failed to show up one morning. She called to say that her ulcer was bothering her and the doctor thought she ought to stay home and rest for a while. She wasn't sure when she'd be well enough to come back.

After she left the telephone, Helen wept. There was anguish for Christy and for herself. Anguish, too, for the lot of women like herself whose early careers did not depend upon their personal gifts or even the state of their own professional market, but on the services provided by Child Care Industries Incorporated.

Mrs. Johnson was followed by Martha Williams in the succession of nannies for Christy. And Christy is now twenty months old. Mrs. Williams has four children of her own. She is a decent, kindly woman, in her thirties, overburdened by the strains of raising her own family without a husband. When one of her own children is ill, Mrs. Williams must stay home. When Mrs. Williams stays home, one of the Andersons must stay home from work. Most frequently it is Helen herself. It is an uneasy plan. Mrs. Williams is wondering whether it might not be better for her to go on welfare until her children are a little older. The Andersons are bracing themselves for another change.

From all this we can see that the options in child care for the affluent Andersons are not really much better than those of the Neustadts. However, since Helen's income is not a critical issue in the Anderson family, Helen has more alternatives open to her.

If her own professional needs seem imperative to her she can examine the options within her community for a stable child-care plan. If her own high standards of child care can be met by a day-care center she may consider that a first rate day-care center with a trained professional staff might provide more stability and continuity of care than the procession of nannies who have entered Christy's life. She may find, however, that "at any price" such a day-care center does not exist in her community. What Helen would ask for in substitute mother care is found in a handful of model nurseries throughout the country, which provide highly trained personnel for their children and adhere to a philosophy of child care which values intimate human connections between a baby and parents, a baby and substitute parents.

It is not cost alone which keeps such model nurseries from proliferating. To operate such model nurseries we would need approximately 2,000,000 professionally trained teachers and aides to serve as mother-substitutes for children under the age of six whose mothers are employed. Substitute mothers with these qualifications are in short supply.

And Helen has other options. If a stable child-care plan at home or at a nursery cannot be worked out, Helen can assess her baby's needs and her own professional needs and make rational choices. She may choose to work part-time for the next two years, which would give her better options in child care since there are more women available for child care on a part-time basis than full time. (Helen is also working in a profession which is accommodating to part-time employment both for women and for men.) Or Helen may choose to stay home until Christy is three and can be enrolled in nursery school while Helen works part-time. (Good half-day preschool programs for the three-to-five-year olds are generally more available and, as we have seen, the preschool child can not only manage separations from his mother for a half day but can profit from his experiences in a good nursery school.)

In summary: The affluent family is not better served than the marginal family by Child Care Industries Incorporated. But the mother whose income is not critical for maintaining the family has the freedom of making rational choices on behalf of herself and her children.

### The Martins: "Who Takes Care of the Caretaker's Children?"

Barbara Martin, whom we met as the aide in charge of the infant nursery at Merry Mites, has her own story. She lives in the Looking Glass World of Day Care in which hundreds of thousands of mothers on welfare take care of the children of hundreds of thousands of working mothers and other mothers on welfare, while hundreds of thousands of women take care of the children of the mothers who are taking care of the children of mothers on welfare and other mothers.[5]

(If this sentence causes dizziness, I recommend that it be read slowly as you turn. With each full rotation, fix your eyes on a distant point. I myself use the dome of Capitol Hill.)

Barbara is the mother of three children, Margaret, ten; Charles, seven; May Ellen, four. Barbara's husband deserted the family four years ago. The family is black. In 1971, Barbara and the three children received an AFDC allowance of $370.00 per month. This covered rent, utilities, clothing, and food for four.*

In 1972 public outrage at welfare costs reached a high pitch. It was an election year and our Christian spirit (banish poverty) wrestled with old devils (the welfare cheater, the squanderer of public funds, the shiftless breadwinner, the AFDC mother who procreates in order to increase her wel-

---

*This provides an annual AFDC income of $4,440 per year. The poverty line for a family of four in the Martin's community was $5,000 per year in 1972.

fare check). It was also the year in which a group
of the nation's statesmen conspired to raise the
price of the children's milk in order to re-elect the
president who employed our public funds to improve the quality of his life. It was not a good year
for Christians or for the Republic. Defense costs
were rising; there were warnings of inflation. It
became increasingly clear that the reason our economy was in danger and public morality at the lowest point in modern history was that Barbara
Martin and her three children were draining our
national resources and our public purse. One of
the nation's highest priorities was to get the Martins off the welfare rolls. "Mandatory employment
of welfare heads of family" and "Work Incentive
Programs" were slogans of the day. (Recall that
75 percent of AFDC heads of families are mothers.)

Around the time that Barbara Martin and
her three children were found to be the cause of
our national decline, Barbara was a full-time
mother. And doing a decent job of it. Like most
welfare mothers I have known, she cared about her
kids and they cared about her. She was a no-non-
sense sort of person and she kept a sharp eye on
her kids as they dodged the neighborhood toughs
and the junkies on the street.

Early in 1973 Barbara was placed in a Work
Incentive Program with the acronym WIN.[6] She
was to receive job training and a chance to improve the quality of her life. The children were
placed in a day-care center, subsidized by federal
funds.

Since Barbara, like most WIN mothers, had
less than a high-school education there weren't too
many career choices open to her. She could be
trained for restaurant kitchen work (average pay

$2.00 per hour) or she could be trained as a child-care aide (average pay $2.00 per hour). Barbara liked children and thought the working hours might be better for a mother in child care than in kitchen work.

In her job training Barbara had a course in child development in which an instructor stressed the importance of the one-to-one relationship in working with small children. And Barbara graduated, and she got a job at Merry Mites, where she alone supervised ten babies between the ages of three months and three years, and she earned $2.00 per hour.

In 1975 May Ellen, four, spent eleven hours a day in a subsidized day-care center. Margaret, ten, and Charles, seven, spent the after-school hours in a subsidized day-care center. The taxpayer's subsidy for the day-care of the three Martin children amounted to $346.00 per month. May Ellen's day-care center was rated "fair," "largely custodial," but it included one hour a day of "cognitive enrichment." The after-school day-care center attended by Margaret and Charles was rated "fair" and, with twenty children supervised by one harassed aide, we must assume that the children provided their own cognitive enrichment.

When Barbara picked up May Ellen at 6:00, she found her four-year-old very cranky because she hadn't seen her mother since 7:00 in the morning. After a full day with ten cranky babies and toddlers, Barbara found that her own kids got on her nerves, and she hated to admit it. Meals were pick-up because Barbara didn't have time to shop regularly, and her apartment refrigerator didn't hold more than two days' food.

And the Martins were still on welfare! They

received supplementary AFDC assistance of $303.80 per month to bring them to the level of the lower-budget Federal Standards.

To explain this we have to go through the Looking Glass.

## THE LOOKING GLASS ECONOMY

It is only natural that when I pass through the Looking Glass I find myself on a platform wearing my unpressed academic gown, and that a class materializes before my eyes. I recognize Alice, the White Queen, and the Red Queen. The blackboard behind me is covered with figures and calculations all carefully set down in mirror writing, including the label " BUDGET ".

"Then how does it happen," asks Alice, "that if Barbara Martin is working, the Martins are still on welfare?" There is a pointer waiting for me, and I begin an explication of the figures on the board.

"In Column I, you will see that if Barbara Martin was not employed she would receive in 1975 a monthly AFDC allowance of $426.40 for her three children and herself. This would cover rent, utilities, food, household necessities, and clothing for four people.

"In Column II, Barbara has graduated from the WIN (Work Incentive) program and has a net income of $317.60 per month after F.I.C.A. and taxes are deducted. This is $108.80 less per month than the family support from AFDC and would not provide a Work Incentive. If Barbara had to assume the costs of day-care for her three children, which comes to $347 per month, and her own costs of employment, estimated at $40 per month, the family income would be wiped out.

"Clearly, then, Barbara and her family will need income supplementation from AFDC and a Work Incentive. Therefore, AFDC must cover (a) the deficit in family income, (b) Barbara's costs of employment, and (c) costs of child care for the employed mother. But these are costs which would not occur if Barbara were not working. Therefore the AFDC provides an additional incentive which is called 'Income Disregard.' This is a form of 'not counting,' and this figure is arrived at by a method of calculation that I will not present to you until you enroll in my Advanced Seminar.

"Now, in computing the AFDC supplementary cash income, the Martins will get the difference between Barbara's net earnings and her former AFDC allowance, *plus* a fraction which constitutes her Work Incentive. The total AFDC cash supplement will be $303.80 per month, but the net gain for Barbara and her children over the former AFDC allowance will be $247.60 per month."

"Then," says Alice, "isn't Something Good Accomplished? I mean like if Barbara Martin is partly self-sufficient and AFDC only has to supplement her income by $303.80, well, isn't that a Saving of $122.60 for the taxpayer?"

"So it would appear, Alice. But scholars who have gone through the Looking Glass and returned have a curious tale to tell. Remember that Barbara Martin's costs of day-care for her three children must be subsidized by the government. If we now add the costs of day-care ($346.60) per month and the cash supplement from AFDC, which is $303.80, we obtain the figure of $650.40, which means that the Federal Government (i.e., the taxpayer) is spending $224.00 *more* per month on the Martin family with Barbara employed than it did when Barbara was unemployed and supporting her family on an AFDC grandt."*

Still," says Alice staunchly, "isn't the Quality of Life improving for the Martins? If the Martins' *net* income is increased by $247.00 per month, isn't that something?"

Alice will surely get an "A" in my course for her nimble mental arithmetic, but I must point out that if the net gain in Barbara's income improves her living standards, we could improve the quality of her life and that of her children by simply adding $100 plus to her cash AFDC allowance while Barbara stays home with her children. The taxpayer, in our computation, would still come out ahead, the children would have their mother's care, and the Martins would be above the poverty line.

"Treachery!" cries the Red Queen. "That would be a Guaranteed Income and that is illegal, unconstitutional, and contrary to the Looking Glass way of life." This is greeted by applause.

The class is getting out of hand. "Ladies and Gentlemen," I say, above the din, *"this is a class in Child Development. Our primary concern is the*

---

*From *The Detroit News,* Tuesday, October 24th, 1972, p. 3A, "Few Good Posts for ADC Mothers: Job Plan's Net Loss Is 3.2 Million," by Don Ball.

"The jobs do not pay enough for the ADC recipient to earn her way off welfare and do not provide promotional opportunity so that she can eventually achieve a salary which would make her independent of the ADC. Instead, her ADC is continued as she works, with the government paying her employment expenses and child care costs.

"Michigan ADC payments were reduced an estimated $1.2 million in the 1970–71 fiscal year because of earnings by ADC recipients who found jobs through WIN programs. But for the same period, the federal government paid $4.6 million more than if the ADC recipients had stayed at home. In other words, the taxpayers were out an overall $3.2 million as a result of the WIN program in Michigan during the 1970–71 fiscal year."

*child and his family and the effects of the Looking
Glass Economy upon the developing child."*

Alice, who sees an "A" in her future, raises
her hand. "Enrichment," she says. "May Ellen is
getting one hour a day of Cognitive Enrichment in
her nursery school. That's a plus. For development, I mean."

"That may be true," I say, "but if May Ellen
can profit from one hour a day of Cognitive Enrichment (and who can't in these melancholy
times), does she need ten more hours a day to
consolidate this learning? And when does the plus
become a minus for the four-year-old girl who still
needs her mother?"

"Are you against Cognitive Enrichment?" It's
the White Queen. (I place an "Ǝ" in my book for
her.) "I am *for* Cognitive Enrichment," I say. "I
am also in favor of Emotional Enrichment. They
go together. In fact, it has been proved that they
*must* go together. I most respectfully urge Your
Majesty to consult the text which has been provided for this course.

"Your Ministry of Child Development has discovered, after spending millions of dollars on research, that mental and emotional development
cannot be separated. You cannot add 'cognitive enrichment' like a vitamin supplement to a child's
daily needs. The child who thrives is the child who
has *both* the nutriments for love and the nutriments
for learning. If we can all agree that Barbara Martin is at least an adequate mother, then she is the
most certain source of those emotional supplies for
her child. No one has yet claimed that May Ellen's nursery school director and her four aides will
give as much love, or more love, or better love than
May Ellen's mother.

"So, if we are only considering May Ellen and her developmental needs, she could profit from a half-day in nursery school (most children do) with a good educational program, and the balance of the day with her mother. This would cost the taxpayer about half the present costs of the eleven-hour-day nursery care and May Ellen would get what she deserves—the best of both worlds.

"May Ellen spends eleven hours each day in a subsidized nursery only because your Ministry of the Budget has persuaded the taxpayer that he is saving money while he is actually losing money. Your Ministry of Child Development has spent millions of dollars to discover that maternal love is one of the great national resources which can still be provided without cost to the taxpayer, and without immediate danger of depletion. And Your Majesty herself has claimed on ceremonial occasions that Our Children Are Our Greatest National Resource."

Alice's hand is raised again. "You haven't said a word yet about some preschool children who might get more from being in a day-care center all day then being at home."

"Well, then, I should," I agree. "Because there are some small children who suffer such emotional impoverishment and instability in their homes that a first rate day-care staff might compensate in some measure for the deficits at home. And then there are small children like Anthony Neustadt. His parents are perfectly adequate, but as long as his mother *must* work, a first rate day-care nursery would be preferable to the revolving-door sitters who appeared in his life in a one-year period. But we've examined the Neustadts' options. And there are no good solutions."

Alice's hand is waving. Urgently. A groan arises from the class.

"What I don't understand," she says, "is what a mother is supposed to *do*. You haven't given any answers at all in this class."

"That," I say, "is because I don't have the answers. I only have the questions.

"That means: If a mother of an infant or pre-school child can freely choose to work or not to work, she can ask herself the questions. If she chooses to work full time for personal reasons, or career reasons, she can examine her options in terms of her child's needs and her own needs and make her decision on the basis of the best information available to her and the real choices she has in substitute care.

"If she *must* work for financial reasons, her options for substitute care are poor and there are almost no good solutions open to her—at least so far—which serve the needs of her child.

"I am worried about millions of children who are being served by Child Care Industries Incorporated. I worry about babies and small children who are delivered like packages to neighbors, to strangers, to storage houses like Merry Mites. In the years when a baby and his parents make their first enduring human partnerships, when love, trust, joy, and self-evaluation emerge through the nurturing love of human partners, millions of small children in our land may be learning values for survival in our baby banks. They may learn the rude justice of the communal playpen. They may learn that the world outside of the home is an indifferent world, or even a hostile world. Or they may learn that all adults are interchangeable, that love is capricious, that human attachment is a perilous investment, and that love should be hoarded for the self in the service of survival."

A sound like the surf at high-tide is rising in the room. Is the Looking Glass World dissolving? No, it is only the sound of shuffling feet and the gathering of papers and books. I recognize it instantly. The class hour has come to an end.

# V

---

## Priorities
## for Children

In this century we have come into knowledge
about childhood and the constitution of personality
that can be fairly placed among the greatest scientific discoveries in history. But the children themselves are not yet the beneficiaries of our science.
Our juvenile laws are chained to archaic principles,
and the social policies which govern the welfare of
children are shaped by the needs of the moment,
or the budgetary crisis of the year. They are blind to
the psychological needs of the child and his family.

In this chapter, I propose to examine certain
aspects of child welfare law and social policy in relation to the central question of this book, the nurturing of human bonds.

### THE SCIENTIFIC LEGACY

It is now over seventy years since Freud discovered that the most severe and crippling emo-

tional disorders of adult life have their genesis in early childhood. During the past thirty years our studies have led us deeper and deeper into the unknown territories of childhood, into infancy and early childhood and the origins of personality. We now know that those qualities that we call "human"—the capacity for enduring love and the exercise of conscience—are not given in human biology; they are the achievement of the earliest human partnership, that between a child and his parents.

And we now know that a child who is deprived of human partners in the early years of life, or who has known shifting or unstable partnerships in the formative period of personality, may suffer permanent impairment in his capacity to love, to learn, to judge, and to abide by the laws of the human community. This child, in effect, has been deprived of his humanity.

How we learned this has been described in Chapter II. It was a discovery that emerged from the wreckage of World War II. The lost children, the abandoned children, the children of Hitler's camps, and the babies without mothers brought about an impassioned inquiry on the part of scientists into the meaning of war to children. What emerged from this inquiry was that even the life-threatening dangers of war were not as destructive to the minds and emotions of children as separation from their mothers and fathers. For many of these children the damage to personality was permanent, even though some of them were later reunited with their parents.

At the war's end, the scientific inquiry moved ahead. It is not only in times of war that children are deprived of mothering and family nurture.

There are circumstances today in which tens of thousands of children in our country are deprived of a mother or a mother substitute. Small children in institutions, children in foster homes, children in storage while their mothers work, and children in their own homes with unstable partnerships form a vast population of sufferers.

As scientists from a number of disciplines examined the effects of maternal deprivation on the developing personality, a consensus of findings emerged. We learned that the developing ego of the young child is inextricably interwoven with the maintenance of the early love bonds and that deprivation of these bonds, or a rupture of bonds already formed, can have permanent effects upon the later capacities of the child to love and to learn. We also learned, from the clinical side of the inquiry, that the most severe and intractable emotional diseases of childhood are the diseases of nonattachment and of broken attachments. A commitment to love is normally given in the early years of life, the gift of ordinary parents, without benefit of psychiatric consultation. But a child who at school age has not yet received this gift may require the whole of our colossal apparatus of psychiatric clinics and remedial education to help him to love and to learn.

These are the extreme cases, yet the number of such children is growing year by year. There are also less virulent but ominous forms of the same disease that are afflicting tens of thousands of other children in our country.

The children of poverty know lost and broken human connections to a frightening degree. There is the father who is not now present or who has never been. There is the mother who works at an ill-paid job and whose babies and young children are delivered like small packages to the doorsteps of neighbors, relatives, day-care centers—"anyone handy"—as it happens in the desperate child-care plans of the poor.

And finally, over the months and years there is no one in this ghostly procession who is mother or stands in the place of mother and no one to bestow identity upon a child. When Head Start began, its teachers were astonished to discover that there were children aged four or five who did not know their own names.

All of this tells us that during the thirty years in which our scientific world made revolutionary discoveries regarding the nature and origin of human bonds and the origins of the diseases of nonattachment, the children themselves have not been the beneficiaries of these discoveries. We have identified a group of malignant diseases of personality, disturbances of the primary human attachments. These diseases are preventable at the source. In a rational world, an army of mental health workers and citizens would gather together to ensure the human bonds of children, to guarantee their human rights.

The mending of children's lives is a very large part of the work of my profession. It would be folly to say that *all* childhood disturbances of personality can be prevented, but a large number that I have seen could have been prevented; and in nearly every case these have been caused by disturbances in the primary human relationships during the early months and years of life.

We have traditionally considered child psychotherapy as a form of prevention. And so it is. If we are successful in treating the childhood form of the neurosis, we may prevent the crippling neuroses of later life. But prevention must be seen in social terms as well. For every child who has been cured of enuresis, bogey men, and youthful pilfering, there are thousands of children waiting, already endangered or damaged because our social institutions and our social policies have robbed them of some measure of their humanity. In the most terrible irony, the mental health professions have been witnesses and sometimes even unwilling collaborators in the tragedy.

## THE DEPARTMENT OF SOMA AND THE DEPARTMENT OF PSYCHE

The history of social work as a mental health profession has cruel paradoxes and many lessons for us.

In the 1920's social workers were among the first to see the implications of Freud's theory of the infantile neurosis for the prevention of adult mental disturbances. In collaboration with psychiatry and psychology they set up child guidance clinics for the identification and treatment of the emotional disturbances of childhood.

The child guidance movement had barely entered its first decade when the disaster of the Great Depression occurred. Poverty, hunger, the emasculation of jobless fathers, desertion of families by broken men, and the placement of children in foster homes were the problems that flooded social agencies and clinics. Social work was also responsible for the development and administration of new programs of public assistance. It was during the period 1935–1939 that a strange bureaucratic marriage was initiated.

The child was divided in accordance with the ancient dichotomy of soma and psyche. The soma of the child was given to the public assistance agencies to be fed and sheltered, and the psyche was given to the child guidance clinic. In the Department of Soma, social workers collaborated with legislators to bring forth the first federal public assistance programs for dependent children (Aid to Dependent Children). This was a remarkable achievement in itself for it guaranteed the subsistence needs of hundreds of thousands of children. But in order to feed the child, they compromised with intransigent legislators and wrote into the enabling laws certain eligibility requirements which have had their effects upon the psyche of the child for over thirty years. The model ADC child would have no father, an absent father, or a disabled father. In all cases, the family that qualified for ADC received higher relief allowances than a family might receive from local welfare sources. This meant, of course, that the family which had an absent father was rewarded by the system and the system of rewards was so effective over three decades that it helped to institutionalize the family without a father among the poor.

The lesson can be summarized in briefest terms: at the same period in the history of social work that brought forth new programs for child mental health, the profession launched and administered public assistance programs which eroded family structure. On one side of the street we had the Department of Soma, issuing mental health problems along with its relief check. On the other side of the street we had the Department of Psyche rapidly expanding its waiting list. In the classic image of Penelope, we wove our cloth by day and unraveled it by night.

The ghost of Penelope haunts the child guidance movement. History records that during the second, third, and fourth decades of our crusade for child mental health there were three wars. For half of those years tens of thousands of children in our country were reared in the family chaos bred by war, and the result was the steady erosion of family bonds, which is the only certain and predictable outcome of war. If the era of child mental health has not brought large rewards to the children, we must reflect that mental health cannot be sustained by clinics alone.

The irony is underscored. These thirty years of intermittent war are the thirty years which gave us the research on the origins of love and the origins of human bonds.

As custodians of this scientific treasure the mental health professions have somehow failed to share the wealth among the social institutions that serve children. Our juvenile courts, as we saw in Chapter III, are privileged to make decisions regarding custody and social treatment for tens of thousands of children. The mental health principles upon which they base their decisions were laid down in the Old Testament. In 1976 the child can remain the property of his natural parents even though they may be strangers to him.

Many thousands of babies and young children spend the early years of their lives in a succession of foster homes and institutions while decisions regarding surrender and custody drag through the courts. The court is empowered to act in the best interests of the child. Since the best interests of the child are incontestably served through sustaining stable human partnerships for the child, the power to act decisively to protect the child and his future surely resides within the law.

These unwanted children who have never known stability or continuity in human partnerships fill the waiting lists of our child guidance clinics and psychiatric hospitals. In truth, they are not wanted there either, for no one has yet invented a treatment that fills the vacancy in personality which occurs when no human partners have entered.

The archaic principle of ownership prevails strangely in another group of custody cases. There are children whose lives as well as psyches are endangered if they remain in their homes with their criminally psychotic parents. But today, even as it was fifty years ago, the court is loath to take protective custody of children who are the property of deranged parents. These children, too, are brought to the doors of the child guidance clinics. But we have not yet found a cure for children whose nightmares are real.

And finally since no one has yet banished Penelope from the social policies that affect children, we have come full circle on poverty too. Since 1936 we have rewarded the families that had an absent father. Since 1967 we have inaugurated relief policies which reward the welfare mother who works and penalizes the mother who doesn't work. Since our government has also closed the door on bills for the development of "quality" daycare facilities, we are now creating an expanded population of little wanderers who are already arriving at the doors of mental health agencies.

We have become partners in a surrealist charade in which society assaults the developing ego of the child and charges the child guidance clinic with the responsibility for repairing it.

## ON POVERTY, THE FAMILY, AND HUMAN BONDS

If the ghost of Penelope has haunted these pages, it is only fair to ask how she got into this story.

At the Child Development Project, University of Michigan, we provide psychiatric services for families with babies and very young children. Most of our patients are the children of poverty. Across the street from us is the County Department of Social Services which administers the AFDC* program and licenses day-care facilities. In children's services in our county, we belong to the Department of Psyche; they belong to the Department of Soma. We are supported by a grant from the National Institute of Mental Health, U.S. Department of Health, Education and Welfare; they too are supported by the U.S. Department of Health, Education and Welfare and the State of Michigan. To the best of my knowledge, the highest policy makers in Washington in the Department of Soma have rarely met the highest policy makers in the Department of Psyche.

In fact, as we have seen, the taxpayer supports two divisions in HEW: one to impair the development of children and another to repair it. Or, if you prefer, one to weave and one to unravel.

---

*In 1950 the ADC program was modified to include payment to the mothers of these families and was renamed Aid to Families of Dependent Children (AFDC).

It is worth mentioning that the larger part of the budget goes into weaving and the smaller into unraveling. However, the taxpayer doesn't know this, and periodically he cries, "A pox on *both* your houses! Where are the benefits from the fortune that is drained from my purse?"

The Federal Department of Soma has a clear mandate. It is required to minister to the bodily needs of AFDC children, to provide food, shelter, clothing, and health care. It is not required by law to minister to the psychic needs of children. That's not their department.

Since one cannot reproach a bureaucracy for exercising its mandate, I will only ask, for the moment, whether the Department of Soma can actually fulfill its obligations under the law.

Can the nutritional needs of a child be met on an AFDC allowance? In my own area, Washtenaw County, Michigan, and in New York City, two high-cost communities which provide high levels of AFDC support, the maximum food allowance is the same: $1.38 per day per person for a family of four. This figure includes food stamp values. Since food costs are 7 percent higher in New York City than in Washtenaw County, the New York City AFDC food allowance is less than our own.

It is conceivable that a nutritionist with expert knowledge of low-cost food exchange values and expertness in marketing could provide nutritional adequacy for a child on this budget; most of us could not. There are many regions in our country which provide much lower levels of support for AFDC children. This means that malnutrition is virtually guaranteed for large numbers of AFDC children.

Poor nutrition *in utero* and during the early years of childhood can create irreversible effects upon all bodily systems. It is directly related to birth defects, serious health problems, and impaired learning. The Department of Soma finds itself in the extraordinary position of inventing new health problems with each relief check.

The free health care available to welfare families is generally of the poorest quality in nearly every community I know. Medicaid (which by 1976 had become the subject of public scandal for widespread fraud within the medical professions and for abuses which have cruelly affected the welfare recipients) has not delivered quality health care on the scale which is necessary to prevent and treat the alarming incidence of illness and death among children of poverty and the debilitating effects upon health of poor nutrition and environmental hazards which affect every child who lives in poverty. Infant mortality rates in the United States are now higher than those of sixteen other countries. Non-white children in our country rank 31st compared to the mortality rates of other countries.[1]

As for the shelter of the body which is furnished by the welfare department, it will virtually guarantee that a child will be reared in a slum dwelling and that he will learn survival tactics in a jungle while he is still a toddler.

However, the subject of this volume is human attachments, so, with a strong warning to myself to keep to the subject, I will now try to examine those policies of public assistance which affect the development of human bonds in the early years of life.

**The Invisible Father**

We have already seen in my brief historical summary that welfare policies have favored the development of female-headed, one-parent families. And while there are many factors that have contributed to this trend in all sectors of our society, there is probably no other condition in our society outside of public assistance (and imprisonment) in which the absence of a father is a requirement and not a choice. This means, of course, that the child in poverty, already disadvantaged by meager sustenance, is deprived of a father or a father substitute—if his mother complies strictly with the rules of eligibility.

Since few young mothers will elect celibacy in exchange for AFDC eligibility, an AFDC household may include a male visitor who serves as father surrogate (or may, in fact, be the "absent" father), and his presence or his connection with the family must be a well-kept family secret. Since harboring a male in an AFDC family is nearly as dangerous as sheltering a fugitive from justice, the male visitor or the surrogate father is, for the children, the center of a shady family conspiracy.

For those who share the old-fashioned view that fathers are central persons in a child's development, a sneak-in and sneak-out father or surrogate father does not provide an elevating model for the children. Also, since his status in the family is uncertain and he may have no real privileges in child rearing, both the attachment between him and the children and the beneficial uses of that attachment in the rearing and discipline of the children may be lost in the family. Further, if one holds to the old-fashioned view that patterns of parenting are transmitted to children through the parental model, we can argue that this model becomes a strong factor in the repetition of one-parent families through generations.

It is the mother, then, who is the central person of a typical AFDC family. In 1975 over 75 percent of AFDC heads of families were women. Since the total number of AFDC recipients is eleven million, and since eight million of these are children,[2] approximately six million children on welfare belong to families in which the mother is the head.

## The "Welfare Mother"

The phrase "welfare mother" now enters our story and requires a brief digression. Since everything that follows will conjure up pictures in our heads, it is important to sort out the pictures. My pictures, which derive from a large experience with "welfare mothers," are not the same as my neighbor's, or that of many public spokesmen, or even of the debaters in Congress. In the public image "the welfare mother" is believed to be profligate with public funds, canny in getting the most out of the system. In heated congressional debate she has been accused more than once of "breeding children out of wedlock in order to extort money from the taxpayer." It is thought by many that she is incapable of rearing children.

In my own large experience with "welfare mothers" it is the rare woman who fits any one of these stereotypes. In Washtenaw County, which is really a large metropolitan community, and in our program, which serves a large number of county families in poverty, we have a fair cross-section of welfare families, black and white. Their babies and young children are in trouble, or they wouldn't be seeing us, and in this respect we should note that so are a large number of middle class families with babies and young children and that's why they are seeing us.

What we see among the "welfare mothers" are large numbers of women who are willing, and able, to make extraordinary personal sacrifices for their children, who show devotion and love for their children under circumstances that cruelly test the quality of maternal love. We see in them hopes and daydreams for their babies and young children which distinguish them in no way from economically advantaged parents. And we do not even understand where the hopes and the daydreams come from.

When we visit them in their bleak and horrible apartments, see them wrestle with the blind bureaucracy that issues the relief check (not always on time), witness a meal that leaves every child hungry and ill-nourished, sit with them for hours in clinics where they and their children are ill-served and degraded, we can only ask ourselves how they have found resources within themselves to meet each day.

A few of these mothers (actually very few—we should note for later reference in this story) are themselves the children of welfare. When we listen to their life stories in which childhood poverty, absent parents, street tyranny, and school failure have brought them full circle to the conditions which are now re-created for their children, we cannot imagine how the human spirit can survive such assaults and yet generate dreams for the children.

Nor are they as a group "hopeless cases." A very large number of our "welfare mothers" have used our help for themselves and their babies. The babies are thriving; their mothers have found new pleasures in their children, a heightened self-regard, and hope for themselves. The majority will not be on welfare long; some are already moving toward employment as the children reach the age of nursery school and grade school. In this respect, we should not take full credit as a psychiatric unit. Welfare, for the majority of AFDC welfare families, is a way station, usually during the period when the children are small and the mother has poor alternatives in employment and for child care. I will expand upon this point later.

## 1967: "Mandatory Employment for Welfare Heads of Families"

The original intention of the AFDC program, when it was inaugurated in 1936 as ADC, was to provide basic support for the children and to encourage mothers to stay home with their children instead of seeking employment to support their families. In 1967 this policy underwent a total reversal. As welfare rolls and welfare costs rose to new heights, there was a great push in Congress to get "welfare heads of families" into jobs, and job training and the work incentive program, WIN, was inaugurated in the Johnson administration. The 1967 Social Security Amendments established programs to encourage welfare mothers to become self-supporting. *Compulsory* work requirements and job training were written into the law, penalties for mothers who refused to participate were stated clearly (a reduction of the AFDC payment). And the law made no exception for the mothers of small children.

The reasons for this shift in policy are highly

complex. I will try to sort out some of the components in economic, social, and psychological motives.

### Mothers in the Labor Market

First, it is important to remember that the stay-at-home mother who was being supported by public policy in 1936 was no longer a symbol of public virtue. In the Sixties hundreds of thousands of women with children were entering the job market each year. There were voices emerging which claimed work as a right for all women. These voices were mainly those of career women. If the national trend was moving strongly toward employment of mothers, why exempt the welfare mother?

In fact a substantial number of AFDC mothers *were* in the labor force, part time or full time, even in 1967, and because of low earnings needed AFDC supplementation to support their families. They were, of course, counted as AFDC recipients.

The *compulsory* work requirement was addressed to a large number of AFDC women who were believed to be slothful and indifferent toward work and self-support. In the inflamed public imagination there were plenty of jobs "out there" for women who were willing to work. And this may even have been true. However, in the heat of debate neither we nor our congressmen were able to grasp the budget arithmetic which turned real income through employment into a surrealist nightmare for the woman in poverty and for the Government Accounting Office (GAO) and its computers as well.

For illustration we can employ a hypothetical AFDC mother and her three children in Los Angeles in the late Sixties.[3] She was receiving $200 per month in support from AFDC. She had a 10th-grade education, no skills. If pride or a mandatory work requirement had brought her to the necessity for employment, she might have found work in a low-paying service job at $2.00 per hour. Would she then have had the dignity of self-sufficiency? Her gross income per month for a forty-hour week would have been $346. Payroll deductions, work re-lated expenses, and the costs of child care (the last computed at the lowest levels) would have con-sumed $242 of her gross earnings. This would have left $104 for the family as real income to be spread over rent and utilities, food, clothing, and incidentals for four persons. The mother would then have had these alternatives: she could have fed the children and not paid the rent and utilities, or she could have paid the rent and not fed the children, or she could have paid the rent, partly fed the children, and left them to shift for themselves without substitute care while she worked.

If she were to remain on AFDC, the real in-come of the family would be $200 per month and her children would remain in her personal care.

If the AFDC mother chose the debasing al-ternative of welfare, we do not have to impute sloth, cunning, and apathy to her motives. It is just as likely that she was a woman who cared about her children and had the basic intelligence re-quired of all of us to manage 5th-grade arithmetic.

In Congress, however, this lady was not praised because there were just too many of her, and we had even larger budget headaches. While motives for choosing welfare over low-paid work could easily be derived from the budget arith-metic of a family in poverty (and all this informa-

tion was available to our legislators and to the taxpayer) it was a difficult idea to hold onto. There is
nothing that stirs our passions like a page of figures
which reveal an unpalatable truth. Our congressional debates record that the woman who did her
arithmetic and came up with the same answers as
the GAO computers was, nevertheless, transformed
into a harpy who preyed upon the taxpayer. (I
have chosen my language carefully. The language
employed in congressional debate was coarser.)

## The Rise in AFDC Rolls and Costs

The other part of the story which led to
reversal of AFDC policy can be stated in straight-
forward terms. Over a decade there was a tremendous rise in the number of families on AFDC,
and the public sosts of welfare were escalating at a
frightening rate. The taxpayer was rebelling, and
his representatives in government were speaking
for him. The phrases "hard core welfare clients"
and "welfare as a way of life" entered public oratory
and drowned out the sober reports of economic
analysts which made the issues more complex and
more perplexing. Since "hard core welfare" in-
flames the imagination and economic studies do
not, it is probably a good idea to take up the
"hard core" issue first.

There is, I am sure, a category of welfare clients who represent the third generation of their
families on welfare. What their numbers are and
whether the incidence of such families on welfare
was or is increasing is a mystery which has not
been illuminated by any of the sources I have con-
sulted. My impression in reading the work of re-
spected scholars in the field is that whatever the

numbers of "hard core" families, they appear *not* to be the cause of the tremendous rise in relief rolls during the past decade.[4]

However, since the whole issue of "hard core welfare" pervades the climate of opinion and muddies our vision of the real problems of poverty, it is worth reporting these facts which bear upon entering and exiting from the welfare system. Sar Levitan, writing in 1971, says, "Steady growth of the (AFDC) rolls masks a tremendous turnover. . . ." "Most families join and leave the AFDC rolls quickly. In recent years approximately one quarter of the cases left within six months; 30 percent left within a year; half closed within two years; and three-fifths within three years."[5]

How to account, then, for the steady rise in welfare rolls? I think there is a fair consensus among social scientists that the rise in relief rolls reflected in large measure social and economic changes and conditions which were affecting the population at large. Thus the increase in the number of families on AFDC reflected the steep rise in the number of female-headed families over the course of a decade, a trend that was seen in all sectors of our society. This increase, in turn, was related to a sharp rise in divorce and desertion rates and the rise in illegitimate births, which increased every year from 1960 to 1968. (The highest increase in illegitimacy was in white births.) To these factors we need to add the rise in the number of women of childbearing age in the general population who had been themselves the babies of the post World War II baby boom.[6] Then, since all women who head families are disadvantaged in the labor market and limited in choice by the needs of dependent children, women with young children and limited education have the poorest options in work, in wages, and in the availability of jobs.[7]

Our wage structure itself failed to provide adequate earnings to sustain a very large number of families in which the head of the family was employed full time. Nearly one out of seven persons employed in 1970 earned less than $2.00 per hour, according to Levitan.[8] If the wage earner was employed full time and supported a family, he could scarcely sustain it above the poverty level. If the wage earner and family head was a woman with young dependent children, the costs of child care would reduce her real income to starvation levels.

We are back, then, to the budget arithmetic which we worked out for the hypothetical Los Angeles mother with three children. The truth was that the rise in the number of AFDC cases reflected economic and social changes which were beyond our grasp in 1970, and are still not fully grasped in 1977.

It would be unnecessary, then, to impute motives of avarice or sloth as reasons for the swelling AFDC caseloads. AFDC actually became the only alternative for large numbers of women with small children.

And a sad and shameful alternative for most of them. Surveys during this period confirmed that the majority of women on AFDC would prefer work to welfare if there were real choices in work and child-care plans. The largest number of AFDC recipients considered welfare shameful and gave heartfelt testimony that the American work ethic was right, that one *should* be self-supporting and not dependent on others.[9] And a substantial number of AFDC mothers (more black than white) were in the labor force, part time or full time, and were still "not making it" without AFDC supplementation.[10]

## How Is Policy Made?

All of this information was available to the policy makers of the Sixties, but policies are not immediately responsive to the knowledge available to us at critical points in the decision-making process. Issues of public welfare stir profound feelings in all of us. Anger, disillusionment, weariness, helplessness, and an urge to take action seize the taxpayer and his elected representatives, and the facts cannot be assimilated. Not right away.

A strong push for action came not alone from the rise in welfare recipients and costs, but public agitation in which "the welfare bum" and "the profligate woman" were marked as the real villains, and these labels drowned out the sober realities of the charts, the tables, and the testimony of experts that the issues were larger and more formidable and lay within the fabric of our economic system and changes in the American family. Wisdom would have dictated postponement of action until it could be guided by solid facts and sound principles. Instead, if I have fairly read the debates of this era, the "hard core welfare family" took on mythic proportions, welfare and hard-core became synonymous, and in anger and desperation we put together a hodgepodge of reforms to save us from the mythical beast who was devouring our house and threatening to set up permanent residence within it.

It was in this climate that we invented our own Creature and named it WIN. As one of the last legacies of The Great Society, the WIN program has proven to be a costly disaster and, like so many legacies of its kind, after nearly a decade of tinkering and patching, it cannot be made to work and cannot even be junked. In the budget arithmetic which I worked out for the Martin family (Chapter IV) you will recall that direct welfare payments were reduced but the costs of child care during job training and employment brought the total costs of the program to a figure that far exceeded the original AFDC payment while the mother remained at home with her children.

On the face of it, it is hard to argue with the idea that welfare families should become self-supporting, that work incentives should be provided to halt the proliferating numbers of families which are being supported through public assistance. If there is no work incentive, it is argued, these families will continue to be sustained at public expense, and larger and larger numbers of families will become dependent upon welfare aid. Already, it has been pointed out, in many states the AFDC payments to families exceed the income of the working poor. And this is true, even though the AFDC support is under the poverty line in every state.

Like any rational person, I too believe that families should have incentives to become self-supporting. But there are six million children in the AFDC families with female heads who require substitute mother care if their mothers are employed, and the services which are provided by Child Care Industries Incorporated do not provide substitute mother care. In fact, as we have seen in Chapter IV, they are, typically, child storage houses, staffed by care-givers who are mostly indifferent and often outrageously neglectful.

Children at all ages are endangered by indifferent care-givers. But children under the age of six are endangered during the most critical period of development. One of the 1967 Social Security Amendments made no exceptions in its compulsory work requirements for the mothers of small children. It is very likely, of course, that there was no intention of enforcing this compulsory work requirement; it was a threat, a legislative temper tantrum, and a wholly dishonest gesture of appeasement to irate congressmen and taxpayers. In practice, in the years that followed, the penalties were not broadly exercised, and discretion in enforcing the work requirement was left to the states. Most states, like my own, do not *require* mothers with children under six to seek job training or employment. But the ambiguities in the law leave much room for "encouragement" and even pressure upon the AFDC mother to seek employment or job training if "suitable child-care arrangements" are available. Since in our state the Department of Social Services is responsible for both the administration of AFDC and the licensing of day-care homes and centers, an extraordinary number of homes and centers have been licensed and judged "suitable." The majority of those I have known would be rated by me as "poor" or even worse.

Then, since the dollar incentives offered to an AFDC mother who works will bring a modest benefit to a family living in extreme poverty (see the budget arithmetic in Chapter IV), there are real incentives to the AFDC mother with small children to seek employment. This combination of "encouragement," subtle threats, and dollar incentives has resulted in a rise in the numbers of AFDC mothers with young children who are employed or in job training throughout the country, and if I can judge the temper of the taxpayer and our legislators, this number may increase each year.

The Department of Soma, then, has complied with the voter's demands that "welfare heads of families" be pushed toward employment and self-support. It has provided incentives and encouragement to mothers to seek employment and it has provided the costs of day care for the children. It has carried out both the voter's mandate and the laws which govern welfare.

### And Then the Children

But the children are not faring well. And that is our department. In the Department of Psyche we are seeing babies and very small children who are not complying with the law. In spite of everything their government is doing for them—jobs for their mothers, day care for themselves, Medicaid, and food stamps—they are not cooperating.

We are seeing an alarming number of babies from AFDC families and other families in poverty who are showing signs of emotional starvation. We see many solemn babies who rarely smile or vocalize. We see some babies who are already developmentally retarded, yet our refined testing may show mental capabilities beyond those reflected in the standard test score. We see babies who do not recognize their mothers at an age where normal babies show recognition and preference for their mothers. A number of these babies are in severe and even life-threatening states of malnutrition.

These are signs and symptoms which are commonly associated with "maternal deprivation." In classic form these signs were first identified in the

18th and 19th centuries in institutionalized infants who were deprived of mothers and mother substitutes.

It would be easy, then, to leap to the generalization that the mothers of these babies in poverty were all guilty of gross neglect, but only in exceptional cases was this found to be so. In our work at the Child Development Project we withhold judgment until all aspects of the baby's life have been examined by us. Our staff is composed of pediatric specialists in medicine, psychiatry, psychology, and social work. Through careful study of these families we made the discovery that many of our most severely endangered babies were children in poverty whose mothers were employed, and who were cared for through the desperate child-care plans of the poor. These included the baby storage home provided by "somebody" in the neighborhood (and sometimes a different "somebody" several times a week) or a baby bank (it could be a child-care center subsidized by the government) in which a procession of indifferent care-givers of doubtful qualifications ministered to twenty babies for ten hours of a baby's day. For all practical purposes, these were motherless babies.

As illustration, I will cite the figures which emerge from one category of severely endangered babies, referred to us for failure-to-thrive (growth failure, no primary physiological causes, associated with severe emotional deprivation). These are babies whose survival is in danger both in the physiological and psychological senses. Among eleven babies referred to us with the diagnosis "failure-to-thrive," ten were in families with incomes below the poverty line. Six of the ten babies in poverty were AFDC recipients. In eight of the eleven cases the mother was not the primary care-giver; she was employed or in job training, and the baby was being cared for in homes or day-care centers, licensed and unlicensed, in each case unable to provide substitute mother care as judged by us. In some cases this was due to indifference and gross neglect in substitute mother care; in others it was the incapacity in a crowded day-care center to provide for the physical and emotional needs of infants and young children.

In this life-threatening disorder we can see that poverty has placed these babies in double jeopardy. First, it will virtually guarantee nutritional inadequacy. Second, in the event that the mother must work, poverty deprives the mother of decent options in substitute mother care and most frequently reduces her options to baby storage places. The result, in such extreme cases as "failure-to-thrive," is a baby who is suffering both a severe nutritional disorder and a severe psychological disorder.

I have used "failure-to-thrive" as a small model for study in this illustration. The majority of the infants in our program who show disorders of attachment have not reached the alarming state of growth failure. But in a very considerable number of cases in which we see disorders of attachment, poverty and the miserable choices imposed upon the poor have brought babies and young children into the care of indifferent and even abusive substitute care arrangements which can be beyond the control of the mother herself.

In speaking of poverty and its effects upon this subgroup of imperiled babies—or any others—

there is no reason to distinguish between the poverty of AFDC (the so-called "dependent poor") and the poverty of the "working poor" who do not seek financial aid. The effects upon the children are not easily discriminated, although it must be said that the children of the working poor will be spared some measure of the degradation and humiliation of poverty which every "welfare child" will know as soon as identity and consciousness of self begin to emerge in his development. And it is a solemn thought, as we pursue certain issues of poverty in these pages, that there are as many families among the "working poor," living below the poverty line, as there are families in the class of the "dependent poor," who are also living below the poverty line.

If I now return to issues of "public policy" and their effects upon children, I am mindful of the fact that poverty can reflect public policy whether the policy is institutionalized, as in welfare, or sanctioned as a kind of personal privilege, in the case of the working poor. In either case, so far as children are concerned, the policy, whether implicit or explicit, is one of indifference to the nation's children.

I have chosen to pursue the issues of public *welfare* policy chiefly because an institutionalized policy provides the most economical route into issues, biases, beliefs, myths, rationalizations, and self-deceptions. It registers as law and written policy and recorded debate and cannot be denied or put out of mind as readily as the unwritten policies which govern our opinions. If we are interested in examining policies which affect the children of poverty, our public welfare policies become a useful guide into the interior.

## WHO ARE THE POLICY MAKERS?

If the reader will agree with me that such AFDC policies can adversely affect the minds and bodies of children, that they can erode the vital human ties between small children and their families, then we must ask, "How did this nation, which loves its children, bring itself to this alarming state? Who are the policy makers who deprive children of emotional and physical sustenance? Who creates a Department of Soma, which assaults the child, and a Department of Psyche to heal him?"

Alas, in our Republic it is the whole lot of us: the taxpayer, the voter, our representatives in government, the bureaucrats, all reflecting, it would appear, a popularly held sentiment. A sentiment *against children?* Not really. How could it be? Since in all the public outrage against The Welfare Mess, nobody ever mentions the children at all.

In the Newspeak which we have all embraced, there is something called Welfare, which is devouring our public purse and cheating the taxpayer. Public outrage is directed toward a group of public enemies called "Welfare Heads of Families." The image which is conjured up is that of a shiftless male, a community bum who could work if he wanted to but prefers to spend the taxpayer's money on booze, or dope, and causes his children to go hungry. Since it is clearly this welfare bum who is starving his children, we, the taxpayers, are not responsible. With each bite the IRS takes from our paychecks, the image of this publicly-supported bum arises like Frankenstein's Monster, and cries for vengeance come to our lips. We write to our newspapers. We write to our congressmen. Get rid of the Welfare Cheaters!

Our congressman has been plagued by this Welfare Bum too, and so he forms committees or joins committees to subdue this monster who is draining our public purse. Periodically, in a cleansing rite which we perform before election, the welfare books are inspected, and it is found that there is bad cheating on welfare going on all over. Auditors report that 5 percent of welfare recipients are ineligible for payments. The careful reader will find that this figure does not represent the incidence of fraud, but an aggregate figure which includes clerical errors in payments or in establishing eligibility. Actual cases of fraud are small in number and the incidence of fraud has changed little over the decades.[11] However, "welfare fraud" is regularly cited in inflammatory prose in our newspapers, and is popularly accepted as a sign of the decline of morals in our Republic. It also has the beneficial and cleansing effect of taking our minds off other frauds.

Being as much a puritan as anybody, I don't like fraud in any form or any place. And I don't think "small frauds" are entitled to apologists any more than "large frauds." So if I now diverge for a moment into the subject of "comparative fraud" I am not concerned about relative proprieties, I only wish to pursue a psychological problem. I am interested in the Welfare Cheater as a durable villain.

The *New York Times* (18 Sept. 1976)[12] reports that a congressional investigation of Medicaid has revealed "widespread fraud and waste" which may amount to as much as 25 to 50 percent of the $15 billion annual expenditures in this program. An earlier story in *Newsweek* (9 Aug. 1976)[13] reported that of the combined Medicaid and Medicare funds amounting to $32 billion annually, "at least ten percent are pilfered annually" as the result of abuses and outright fraud by all segments of the medical profession."

In the year in which these stories were written, 1976, our congressional offices were riddled with scandals. The matrimonial fidelity and moral purpose of a number of statesmen were tested and found wanting by playmates on their office payrolls. These diversions were unknowingly subsidized by the American taxpayer, whose indignation knew no bounds when it was learned that these office bunnies could not type and kept irregular hours.

In this year, too, our national police force, the FBI, was found with a hand in the taxpayer's pocket. Our CIA has devoted a large chunk of the taxpayer's money to burglaries ("unauthorized burglaries," as the phrase goes) and has committed hundreds of millions of the taxpayer's money to the "destabilization" of the governments of foreign countries. With a few blueprints for murder.

When we consider the number and cultural diversity of this gang of rogues and crooks who have been feasting on the taxpayer's money, it is remarkable how durable as a national villain the Welfare Head of the Family has been. Scandals come and go, but on our public enemies list there is really no one else who consistently makes the headlines every day and who can stir our passions to such a frenzy.

Who is he?

I have gone in search of him. In the library stacks. Where else?

Levitan reports: "Although one welfare family in six includes a father, two-thirds of these men are incapacitated; only about five percent of AFDC families include an able-bodied father. More than seven families in ten include only the mother. One family in ten includes neither the father nor the mother, and the children live with a caretaker relative or in a foster home."[14]

The Welfare Bum is apparently hiding out in that 5 percent of AFDC families. However, since a good number of those men may be temporarily unemployed or may, in fact, be working full time or half time at hourly rates that cannot support a family without AFDC supplementation, we have to search further in these figures for the Welfare Bum who refuses to work in order to exploit the taxpayer. Does he represent one percent? Two percent? I cannot find further information. However, even at 2 percent the taxpayer should feel some relief. The incidence of able-bodied men on AFDC who are unwilling to support their families through work (or cannot find work) would not appear to be high enough to threaten the American work ethic.

This leaves us with the problem of identifying the Welfare Heads of Families for our rites of exorcism and, alas, the figures and the gender will not change.

Seventy-five percent of Welfare Heads of Families are women, mothers of dependent children. Since dependent children are by definition in need of a mother's care, these Welfare Heads of Families are not, strictly speaking, unemployed.

The battle cry "mandatory employment for welfare heads of families" has a hollow ring when our public crusaders come charging down the hill to find the shiftless bum who is feasting upon the taxpayer's money and find a woman with three children. And they are not feasting.

Who, then, is stealing the taxpayer's money? Is it the children? Or their mother? Since we are a nation that loves its children we will not accuse them of stealing the taxpayer's money. And since "mother" is a word that evokes the wrong sentiments for tax cutting, we are left without a villain unless we can engage the welfare bum (male) to furnish his valuable services.

It is the children, of course, who are ultimately responsible. Once the children get into the picture they louse up policy decisions. If we keep them in the picture and label them as "welfare recipients" we can't reduce welfare expenditures. We might even have to increase them. And since the children are not spending the taxpayer's money on booze, there is no one to blame for our fiscal crisis and the deterioration of public morals. In order to preserve our economic policies, which call for "drastic cuts in public spending," we have to get the children out of the picture. This can be done through a massive act of repression: there are no children in Aid to Families of Dependent Children. And now, since someone clearly is stealing the taxpayer's money, we discover to our relief that it is the welfare head of family—and the male bum offers himself (with a lewd smirk) for ritual sacrifice.

When the male bum is not available (hired elsewhere; everyone needs him) a carefully selected female counterpart can be employed. In another version of this national soap opera the welfare head of family *is* a woman. The phrase "welfare mother" is deleted from the script because the word "mother" will introduce the wrong sentiments for "mandatory employment." There are still a lot of taxpayers and congressmen who don't like the idea of working *mothers*. But if it can be demonstrated that these female heads of welfare families are unworthy of the sacred name "mother," well then, by God, we and our congressional representatives will support "mandatory employment."

So it is necessary to prove that these women are unworthy. Well, then, a large number of them have conceived their children out of wedlock. They are sinners who should now do penance. (Senatuh, we could all do with a little penance.) And some of these women have continued to procreate while receiving public funds. That makes them *unrepentant* sinners, and they should pay. (Let's send the bill to the children.) And the reason that they procreate and continue to procreate is *in order to get public funds*. (Any unrepentant sinner could figure out an easier way of making a living.) And they let their children go running loose on the streets. (Not proven. But the rental allowance on AFDC does not get the kids a garden apartment.) Anyway, as the picture of a sinful and profligate woman emerges, a woman who neglects her children and profanes the word "mother," it is not difficult for the taxpayer and the congressman to chant in unison, "Get the cheaters off of welfare!" And "mandatory employment of AFDC heads of families" is a shoo-in.

Here, again, the children louse up the script. Somebody, perhaps a bureaucrat who is paid to keep these things in his head, will bring up the question of the children. "What children?" "Those

Dependent Children that we are giving Aid To. If the woman goes to work, who will take care of those Dependent Children?" There is a pause for everyone to collect his thoughts. "Day Care!" someone remembers. He is greeted with a cheer. The children will all go to day-care centers. Nice clean day-care centers with a hot lunch, and teachers who will give them cultural enrichment and keep them off the streets. Then, says the bureaucrat, we will need day-care funds for six million AFDC children whose female heads of family are employed during the day. *That*, says the committee, is inflationary and we will vote against it. The committee adjourns with the recommendation that day care be provided for all children of welfare mothers who are employed and that no new money be appropriated for day-care centers.

The children can now be obliterated from consciousness and conscience. As the ill-served consumers of Child Care Industries Incorporated, they will not complain to their congressmen. They have no vote anyway. They are an invisible constituency in every congressional district.

Finally, it appears that the duplicity which has governed our public policies affecting the welfare of children is not the result of a master plan to defraud the children of basic human needs, but the result of mental trickery in the public conscience. By getting the children out of the picture we are free to pursue our tough-minded policies with respect to public aid and to cut the budget without a tear. With the children out of the picture we can vote for mandatory employment of "welfare heads of families," provide dollar incentives to the AFDC mother who works, and build a costly subsidy for day care. By keeping the direct costs of welfare

allowances in a separate budget from the subsidies,
we console the irate taxpayer. The net additional
costs of this program to the taxpayer can be calculated in the hundreds of millions. The child-care
programs provided for the children have been generally of the poorest quality, although the taxpayer
has paid heavily for storage costs. The costs paid
by the children who are in storage have not been
calculated by anyone.

## ALTERNATIVE POVERTY PROPOSALS

The alternatives to The Welfare Mess have
been various forms of income redistribution plans
in which the welfare apparatus is dismantled and
the poor are provided with a minimum base income which would be accountable through the
mechanisms that already exist in IRS. In principle
it is equitable. It gets rid of the public assistance
caseworkers and functionaries who police the poor
and degrade them, and it leaves the problem of
who is cheating and who is not reporting income
to the IRS, which bring the poor to the same status
as taxpaying citizens that the rest of us enjoy.

However, the fate of Nixon's Family Assistance
Plan is highly instructive to those who seek welfare reform and a plan to eradicate poverty in our
country. The plan, sensibly enough, included income supplements for the "working poor" as well as
the so-called "dependent poor," and evolved from
the concept of a negative income tax. The base levels proposed in the various modifications of this
proposal would not eradicate poverty, but were
conceived as a first step toward a policy of income support and a redistribution of the tax burden. The arithmetic involved would bring us back

into the Looking Glass Economy, and I have no heart to go through the looking glass again.[15]

The Nixon plan was introduced on October 3, 1969. The House approved the plan with some modifications in April 1970. The Senate Finance Committee balked on a number of issues. Liberals felt the level of payments was too low. Many conservatives were against the program from the start and called it "a guaranteed annual income." The arguments circled around the issues of "work incentives," and the Welfare Bum and the Profligate Woman came on stage for their ritual performance.* The arithmetic of work incentives, worked and reworked in endless revisions, never closed the gap in the arguments. And, alas, no arithmetic could cover the gap between the proposals for income support and the prevailing level of support of 90 percent of welfare recipients.[16]

While salvage operations were begun by FAP supporters, another storm broke out—the Cambodian incursion—and FAP was abandoned.

New income redistribution plans are again in preparation as I write the final pages of this chapter. If a wizard appears who can close the gaps in the old plan, or devise a new one, it is safe to predict that the cry "inflationary" will create turmoil once again. And it may take another wizard to get the Welfare Bum and Profligate Woman

---

*Would a negative income tax with graduated work incentives result in a reduced work effort or withdrawal from the labor force? In a recent field experiment conducted in New Jersey (families with a *male* head, the major group not now covered under cash assistance programs) analysis of data covering a three-year period showed no difference in the labor force participation between the experimental and the control group families. *Setting National Priorities*, p. 186.

off the stage in our national soap opera so as to leave a decent space for the children.

In 1974 there were 10.2 million children living in "official" poverty, the term for the federal "poverty line." For a non-farm family of four, the threshold in that year was $5,038. A more accurate measure of poverty based upon Department of Labor minimum income standards would bring the figure to 17 million children who were living on less than the minimum required for basic needs. Of these there were about 5.5 million under the age of six.[17]

## BUDGET PRIORITIES AND PRIORITIES FOR CHILDREN

This has been a long discourse on poverty for a small book dealing with the child and his human bonds. If I have dwelt at length on social welfare policies and their effects upon human attachments, it is because I firmly believe that the children of poverty are the single largest group in our nation which is robbed of its human potential in infancy and the early years.

The children of poverty suffer lost and broken connections in their human partnerships as a commonplace experience: for other children in our society this need not be. I have argued that this is not a wholesale indictment of parents in poverty, rather that poverty robs a parent of the freedom to make the good choices and the wise choices on behalf of children.

A mother on welfare can be provided with all the useful information I have offered in this book on the importance of human attachments (she

may know it without this book) and not be in a
position to employ that knowledge to serve the best
interests of her child. If AFDC policy requires her
to work, or offers incentive to work, her own
knowledge of what her child needs is practically
irrelevant. If the additional income from her low-
paid job provides her child with at least minimum
adequate nutrition, she may have to weigh that
fact against the psychological risks for her baby or
young child. If her earnings at $2.00 or $2.50 per
hour cannot obtain good substitute care for her
child, she will have to settle for less. If the govern-
ment-subsidized day-care center is regarded as
"suitable" by AFDC and "unsuitable" by the mother herself, she may find it prudent to accept the
day-care center. If she finds that her AFDC rental
allowance gives her a rat-infested flat, she must
settle for rats; she is unlikely to find something
better. If her AFDC shelter provides her with
neighbors who are junkies and prostitutes, she is
not likely to escape them through moving. If
she teaches her kids to dodge the junkies and the
street toughs, she will be lucky if one out of three
will learn to dodge them successfully.

The bad choices are obligatory. And they are
supported by public policy.

A rational public policy for children cannot co-
exist with poverty and our current welfare practices. Yet each of the income redistribution plans
which has been proposed to date has created a
storm. "Something for nothing!" "Astronomical
costs!" "Inflationary!" In a year like 1976, for instance, in which our Defense budget was 114 billion dollars,[18] the phrase "astronomical costs" had
a hollow ring.

The cost of maintaining children in poverty

cannot be calculated in dollars and cents. For those who like to work out the figures, I would suggest some of the factors that need to go into the calculation. The lost and broken human connections which are the common lot of many young children in poverty are directly related to the social diseases of poverty. School failure, juvenile crime, mental instability are increased in any population in which the bonds between the child and his human partners are absent or eroded as in the circumstances of poverty. Malnutrition *in utero* and throughout the years of childhood is directly related to the high incidence of disease and early death in the families of poverty. The omnipresent neighborhood dangers and crime which every ghetto child experiences will infect a very large part of the child population and provide irresistible vocational models for the vulnerable. The climate of self-denigration and despair in the ghetto will do the rest. By the time the welfare child has reached the age of six, his net worth in cash and I.Q. will be calculated for him, and he will know it isn't much. If he survives to the age of marriage, he is likely, as the rest of us are, to reproduce the patterns of his child-rearing for his own children.

Someone else will have to go off to the library to get the statistics on the real cost of maintaining poverty for this nation. I think they will be "astronomical," as we say now. If we add these real costs to the dollar costs of our present welfare system, we might discover that a rational "income redistribution plan" is the best bargain of the century.

The ultimate benefits to the economy should also be weighed heavily in the calculation. My friend Harold Shapiro, chairman of the Department of Economics at the University of Michigan, points out that optimal development in childhood is related to future productivity in the labor market. The investment now in family support and the welfare of children could bring incalculable benefits to the economy in the future.

In dollars the costs of an income support program to bring a large segment of our nation out of extreme poverty will be very large: annually in the billions, we can expect.* Another such income proposal will certainly bring cries of agony from the taxpayer. On the other hand, the taxpayer shows a serene passivity in shelling out hundreds of billions for national defense. He can do this under the illusion that every billion is purchasing his security, and the more billions he invests in security the more security he will have.

The costs in billions of providing every child with the biological and psychological necessities for optimal development should not stir national outrage when they are placed beside the costs of insuring our national security. And I am assuming that the costs of a new income program for the poor would continue (like defense) for many years to come. Poverty and the social diseases bred by poverty cannot be abolished in five years or ten years, perhaps not in fifty years. We can consult our history books and learn that massive social reform will not bring about "significant change" until generations have been affected by the minute increments of change which finally accrue as benefits

---

*One estimate by economists: The net Federal costs of an income support program to replace AFDC, food stamps, supplementary security income, etc., and provide an income guarantee of $4,800 for a family of four, would be about $15 billion, calculated in 1976 dollars. Such a program would include about a quarter of the U.S. population, the working poor as well as the dependent poor. *Setting National Priorities*, p. 204.

to a population. For the cost accountants who will demand instant results from the national sacrifice to abolish poverty, there is a warning from us social scientists to put their computers to work on another program for the next forty years and leave the poverty budget to work on its humane mission without computing the cash value of children's lives.

The question, "Can we afford billions to abolish poverty and billions for defense?" falsifies the issues for the voter and the taxpayer. Our budget priorities have gone to defense because the generals have persuaded us that these billions will insure our survival as a people. It can be fairly argued that the highest priority for mankind is to save itself from extinction. However, it can also be argued that a society that neglects its children and robs them of their human potential can extinguish itself without an external enemy.

# VI

## The Tribal Guardians

The legendary angels and benevolent spirits who guide the fortunes of the newborn child are not invited to the christening of a very large number of American babies. In their place we send agents of the bureaucracy, immigration officers, insurance brokers, and cost accountants who examine the credentials of the baby for entering the human community. Now that he's here, should he be here at all? Can he pay his own way? If not, does he intend to live in decent poverty or does he intend to be dependent upon the taxpayers of this community? What are the moral credentials of his parents? Is he the right color for the human race? Has he in general chosen his genetic heritage, his parents, and his socioeconomic status in ways that conform to the high standards required for membership in our society?

It is not good for babies to have immigration officers, insurance brokers, and cost accountants to preside at the christening, and the babies cannot thrive.

To the credit of the celestial agents, they never ask these questions. They are sensible and, considering their habits, down to earth about these things. The baby is *here*, they say with commendable sense. He belongs to all of us. If misfortune has governed the circumstance of his birth, they appoint godparents, seers, sages, and even humble people to guide the fortunes of the baby. In my reading of legends, this kind of social action practiced by the angels has had a highly beneficial effect upon the babies. My analysis of outcome studies, widely dispersed in mythology and sacred texts, shows that the largest number of babies whose destinies have been guided by love and wisdom in a devoted human community have transcended circumstance and returned the gift.

Before I become hopelessly trapped in my allegories—and before I lose the certificate of mental health which is conferred upon me by my profession—I should set the record straight: I do not believe in these celestial spirits; I never believed in them even at an age when I should have. Like any observant child poring over the pictures in my illustrated Grimm's, I soon discovered that all those celestial celebrants at the christening had the same faces as the "real people" who appeared in other illustrations throughout the book. Beneath the wings and the crowns and the robes, and my own jelly smears, I could recognize every one of them. The celebrant in the blue robe and halo was the shoemaker who wore a leather apron and tiny spectacles when the elves visited him. The fellow with the tipsy crown and red robes was the baker who brought white loaves to a virtuous maiden who had been left to die of starvation. The radiant purple angel was the widow who had last seen her only son, a headstrong boy, when he ascended a bean stalk. They were the village folk in fancy dress. They had put aside their sorrows and just grievances with the world to celebrate the birth of a new baby and bring him gifts.

As I understand it now they were representatives of the village or the tribe who followed an ancient tradition in which the parents conferred life upon the child and the community united with the family to insure the human rights of the newborn.

The tradition survives in thousands of small communities throughout the world, including some in our own country. But as cities rise, the ancient bonds of community become tenuous, or are dissolved. The tribal guardians of the child are replaced by institutional guardians. In modern history the institutional guardians are agents of government in health, law, social welfare, and public accounting. Each of them is assigned a piece of the child and his family, and there is no one among them who is assigned the ancient role of celebrant at the birth and guardian of the human rights of the infant. The child and his family are anonymous, and will remain so unless misfortune brings them out of anonymity. There are also bureaus and agents in the department of misfortune.

It can be argued that the largest number of babies and families in megalopolis appear to survive without self-appointed guardians of the child's human rights and tribal celebrants at the birth. Those who do not fare well are victims, we say, of their own inadequacy. But, in fact, I can testify that nearly every young family faces great strain and extraordinary demands upon its internal resources when it brings a new baby into the world. Unaided by relatives and a devoted community, the young family is cast adrift to confer as best it can its own blessings upon the child and the store of its own wisdom. In favor of the ancient tradition, every baby and his family was embraced in the arms of the community, and the strength of the family was augmented a thousand-fold by the bonds of the community. It was a form of mental health insurance. It is conceivable that the community prevented breakdown in many families and thus insured the rights of infants. When it happened that all the blessings and sacred rites did not prevent trouble for a baby, the self-appointed guardians of the baby took their work seriously. They were not impeded by bureaucratic regulations. They brought the best of their wisdom to the endangered baby and his family with the love and authority that only a community can confer upon its members.

All this happens, even today, in a community when babies and their families are not anonymous. The baby belongs to his family, but he is also "our baby."

As a member of the mental health profession I am not suggesting the abolition of my profession in favor of celestial spirits, or paraprofessionals, for the guardianship of the mental health of infants. When a baby is in psychological peril, I would rather have his parents consult me than Great Aunt Sadie. I know more than she does about these things. But I welcome Aunt Sadie as a collaborator if she is the source of emotional sustenance for the family and if the baby is precious to her. We need each other. When, in fact, I am called in to see an imperiled baby in his home I will sometimes find the whole clan assembled there to look me over. They are not in the least interested in my university credentials. They take those for granted. Do I *care* about *their* baby? is what they want to know and they will put me to a rough test. For my part, I see the gathering of the clan, however quarrelsome and self-righteous this clan may be, as a good omen. I am counting on the baby, his parents, and the whole tribe to enable me to do my own work.

What I am saying, then, is that the institutional guardians of the baby's human rights—and I am one of those—can mend, repair, bring wisdom to the cause of babies but cannot take the place of tribal guardians of the baby. Neither can we all return to villages to revive the ancient practices. There must be ways in which a modern urban society can find measures to replace or reconstitute or rediscover the tribal guardians who insure the rights of infants.

Who is out there to take up the cause? Millions, I think. If the tribe is scattered and the guardians are scattered, the love of babies has not been extinguished. In work with needy children and their families, I have found that I have only to mention that something which is not immediately available is needed for a baby, and there may not be enough people to man the switchboard. If I write a piece in a popular magazine describing an unmet need of babies, our office will be snowed under as the letters of concern, the offers of help arrive, and continue to arrive, for weeks.

What I have seen is that when a baby and his

family arise from anonymity because of need or danger, the sense of community is immediately aroused and we are transformed into a village in which every member of the tribe plays a traditional role. The purpose of this book has been to identify babies and their families and their needs and to make them visible. When this happens, the babies become *our* babies, the tribe rallies round, and intelligent solutions can be found.

A nation is a community, too. We are still new in the experiment of democracy and the ways in which our social institutions can respond to need on a vast scale. When the institutions do not serve these needs and may themselves be inventing new social diseases while we are working on the old ones, we spend much of our human energies in repairing and patching, or simply imploring the machines to work (a practice that I employ with my household appliances when they become obstinate). In the case of those institutions that serve children and their families, there is now a colossal apparatus which spans the country and consumes a fortune—and it doesn't work.

I think it doesn't work because there are no governing principles among these institutions, no ideas which give unity and purpose to their programs. They have lost "the human center," to use Erich Kahler's phrase.[1] And when that is lost, the programs themselves can do nothing more than perpetuate themselves, like those monstrous machines that have discovered the secret of self-duplication.

If we take seriously the psychological evidence that emerges from the study of human infancy— and I think we must—there *is* a unifying principle which can govern the social programs which serve families and their children. The principle is found in the primacy of human attachments. If we translate this principle into a creed for the governance of these programs and the services provided by them it might be stated in these words: Every social program in medicine, law, education, and public welfare must commit itself to the protection of the human rights of children, the rights of enduring human partnerships, the right to be cherished by family and community, the right to fully realize their human potentials. The same principle provides useful guidelines for judging the performance of a program and revisions of programs. Thus, if medical practice exerts itself on behalf of the physical well-being of babies and their families but neglects the psychological needs of a child and his parents at birth and after birth, it has not fully protected the human rights of children and must answer to the community. If our laws and our court practices deprive children of their rights through obsolete beliefs and judgments, the laws and their executors must be called to public accounting for ignorance of the psychological needs of children. If our day-care programs and our educational programs ignore the psychological needs of children, or assault these needs through their practices, they must answer to an outraged citizenry. If our programs for families in poverty create conditions in which a child may be starved physically and psychologically, these programs must be abolished, and humane solutions must be found.

"Accountability," which most often today refers to cost accounting, must have the meaning of moral accountability to the public. And the public must itself be an informed public and a public that represents the children's cause.

In this sense we are all guardians of the children's rights. And if the village conditions which conferred tribal guardians upon the newborn and his family do not prevail in a complex society, we can reconstitute the mission of the tribal guardians for a complex society.

The children need spokesmen, advocates, and lobbyists, too, at every level of social and political organization in which public policy and law affect the development of the child and may impinge upon his human rights. On the highest levels of government we need powerful spokesmen for "the special interests" of children who can speak with authority and with the strength of numbers behind them.

The children's cause which is the subject of Gilbert Steiner's book of the same name has more often served other "causes" in Washington than those of the children.[2] As I read Steiner's book (which appeared as I was completing the first draft of this book) I found myself in another Looking Glass world. There have been, and are, many children's causes, nearly all transitory and issue oriented. The spokesmen for the children, also "issue oriented," have themselves been transitory since their mission was either accomplished or was not accomplished. School lunch programs, mandatory education of the handicapped, child abuse, day care, become issues that summon various factions to Washington, to speak for the children, to speak for themselves and *their* causes, to argue among themselves, to form temporary and often grudging coalitions, to disband after victory or defeat.

Thus, to use one example, subsidized day care has brought to Washington an assortment of bedfellows who, under ordinary circumstances, would decline to share an office suite together. There are career women who want subsidized day care as an instrument for their liberation from the home and children. There are welfare mothers who want quality day care for their children while they are working out of economic necessity. There are educators who see day care as an institution for enrichment of the lives of disadvantaged children. Unionists want an expansion of day-care programs for children in order to provide jobs for the large number of excess teachers on the market. Social activists see child development centers as a catalyst for community development and social change.

Since this is the way business is done in our democracy—and it has generally worked well for 200 years—why should one quarrel with this means of conducting business for the children? But self-interest and compromise, which work well for the allocation of funds for regional resources, government contracts, tax proposals, and other domestic issues do not work as well when children and human resources are at stake. In fact, as I have argued elsewhere in this book, self-interest and compromise have themselves been responsible for laws and public policies which have generated new problems for children and their families.

Thus, in the day-care coalition I have described, some of the issue-oriented lobbyists are speaking for their own special interests and some may be speaking out of altruistic motives and love of children, but none of them is asking the disinterested questions: "If the program is enacted will it serve the developmental needs of young children? Will the design of the program insure quality care for children? Does it define 'quality care' and specify how it will be obtained? Will it sustain and strengthen the vital human connections of children? When the compromises have been made by all the special interest groups, will the children be compromised?"

Each of the issue-oriented groups may be assuming that there is somebody else "out there" who will be looking out for those things. But there isn't anybody else out there. Except us.

The virtue of the tribal guardians, the ordinary citizens like ourselves, is that we are not encumbered by "self-interest," and the "issue" is the child himself. An informed citizenry, committed to the rights of children, can ask the difficult questions, read the fine print in the proposal, look for the guarantees of the children's rights and necessities, and refuse compromises if the children's rights are endangered. And each of us holds a ballot in his hands for the citizen who is too young to vote.

Those tribal guardians could be a formidable lobby once they got together.

## Notes

### Chapter I

The literature on mother-infant attachments is vast and dispersed among a large number of journals and books in specialized fields of human and animal psychology. A good summary and discussion of the human and animal literatures will be found in John Bowlby's *Attachment and Loss*. René Spitz's work, *The First Year of Life*, is a valuable introduction to the central issues in the study of human attachment and brings a historical perspective to this study which only one of the great pioneers could provide. Studies of mother-infant bonding in the neonatal period are examined by Marshall Klaus and John Kennell, along with concise presentations of their own ground-breaking research in this area, in their book, *Maternal Infant Bonding*.

Konrad Lorenz's book, *On Aggression* (discussed at some length in Chapter II), is actually a fascinating study of the origins of love and the characteristics of mother-infant attachment in a wide range of species. Jane Van Lawick-Goodall touches upon infant-mother bonding among chimpanzees in "The Behavior of Free Living Chimpanzees in the Gombe Stream Reserve."

Cross-cultural practices in infant rearing which are touched upon in this chapter are still sparsely documented in the anthropological literature. Among the classics in the field which serve as good introductions to the subject are Beatrice Whiting's *Six Cultures: Studies of Child Rearing*, John Whiting and Irvin Child's *Child Training and Personality*, Oscar Lewis's *Life in a Mexican Village*, and Mary Ainsworth's *Infancy in Uganda*, which is devoted entirely to the issues of infant rearing.

1. On the "love language," see the following: Robson, K. S. (1967): "The Role of Eye-to-Eye Contact in Maternal-Infant Attachment." *Journal of Child Psychology and Psychiatry* 8:13–25; Stern, D. (1974): "Mother and Infant at Play: The Dyadic Interaction Involving Facial, Vocal and Gaze Behavior." In Lewis, M., and Rosenblum, L. (eds.), *The Effect of the Infant on Its Caregiver*. New York: Wiley, pp. 187–215; Fraiberg, S. (1974): "Blind Infants and Their Mothers: An Examination of the Sign System," and also pp. 215–233; Spitz, R. A., and Wolf, K. M. (1946): "The Smiling Response: A Contribution to the Ontogenesis of Social Relations." *Genetic Psychology Monographs* 34: 57–125; Emde, R. N., and Koenig, K. L. (1969): "Neonatal Smiling, Frowning, and Rapid Eye Movement States: II, Sleep-Cycle Study."*Journal of the American Academy of Child Psychiatry* 8, 4:637–656.

2. U.S. infant mortality rates are now higher than sixteen other countries'. Non-white Americans rank 31st. *America's Children 1976*. Washington: The National Council of Organizations for Children and Youth, p. 32.

3. Prescott, J. W. (1971): "Early Somatosensory Deprivation as an Ontogenetic Process in the Abnormal Development of the Brain and Behavior." In Goldsmith, I. E., and Moor-Jankowski, J. (eds.), *Medical Primatology 1970*. Basel: Karger, pp. 356–375; Korner, A. F., and Thoman, E. B. (1972): "The Relative Efficacy of Contact and Vestibular-Proprioceptive Stimulation in Soothing Neonates." *Child Development* 43: 443–453; Kulka, A., Fry, C., and Goldstein, F. (1960): "Kinesthetic Needs in Infancy." *American Journal of*

*Orthopsychiatry* 3: 562–571; Frank, L. K. (1957): "Tactile Communication." *Genetic Psychology Monographs* 56: 209–225.

4. Van Lawick-Goodall, J. (1968): "The Behavior of Free-Living Chimpanzees in the Gombe Stream Reserve." In Cullen, J. M., and Beer, C. G. (eds.), *Animal Behavior Monographs* I, 3: 161–311.

5. Kaufman, I. C., and Rosenblum, L. A. (1967): "Depression in Infant Monkeys Separated from their Mothers." *Science* 155: 1030–1.

6. Harlow, H. F. (1959): "Love in Infant Monkeys." *Scientific American* 200: 68–74; Harlow, H. F., and Harlow, M. K. (1965): "The Affectional Systems." In Schrier, A. M., Harlow, H. F., and Stollnitz, F. (eds.): *Behavior of Nonhuman Primates, Vol. 2.* New York: Academic Press, pp. 293–298.

7. Here I am referring to the classic studies of Drs. John Kennell and Marshall Klaus at Case Western Reserve Medical School. They have amassed strong evidence for a "sensitive period" in mother-infant bonding which normally occurs in the first hours and days after birth. Grave disruptions in the conditions for bonding (and hospital practices may constitute a major form of disruption) can impede the process of bonding. Klaus, M. H., and Kennell, J. H. (1976): *Maternal-Infant Bonding (The Impact of Early Separation or Loss on Family Development).* Saint Louis: C. V. Mosby Company.

## Chapter II

1. Lorenz, K. (1967): *On Aggression.* New York: Harcourt, Brace and World.

2. Harlow, H. F., and Harlow, M. K. (1965): "The Affectional Systems." In Schrier, A. M., Harlow, H. F., and Stollnitz, F. (eds.), *Behavior of Nonhuman Primates, Vol. 2.* New York: Academic Press.

3. Freud, Sigmund (1955): "Analysis of a Phobia in a Five-Year-Old Boy." Originally published in 1909, part of the Standard Edition of *The Complete Psychological Works of Sigmund Freud.* London: Hogarth.

4. Capote, Truman (1966): *In Cold Blood*. New York: Random House.

5. We should carefully distinguish this kind of group care from that provided babies and young children in a kibbutz. The kibbutz baby has a mother and is usually breast-fed by her. Studies show that the kibbutz baby is attached to his mother and that the mother remains central in his early development. The group care of the kibbutz does not deprive the baby of mothering, whereas such deprivation is the crucial point of the studies I cite in this essay.

6. Spitz, R. A. (1945): "Hospitalism: An Inquiry into the Genesis of Psychiatric Conditions in Early Childhood." *Psychoanalytic Study of the Child* 1:53–74.

7. Provence, S., and Lipton, R. (1962): *Infants in Institutions*. New York: International Universities Press.

8. Wolff, P. H. (1963): "Observations on the Early Development of Smiling." In Foss, B. M. (ed.), *Determinants of Infant Behavior II*. London: Methuen, pp. 113–138.

9. Spitz, R. A. (1965): *The First Year of Life*. New York: International Universities Press.

10. Freud, A., and Burlingham, D. (1944): *Infants Without Families*. New York: International Universities Press.

## Chapter III

1. 23 *Buffalo Law Review* 1 (1972): "Adoption and Child Custody: Best Interests of the Child," pp. 1–16.

2. *Life*, 1 December, 1972.

3. *New York Times*, 23 February, 1972: " 'Low Moral Standards' Judge Ruled: A Case of Changing Mores" by Laurie Johnston, p. 36.

4. *Jet*, 23 March, 1972: "Black Infant Center" by Warren Brown, pp. 12–15.

5. *The Ann Arbor News*, 17 November, 1976: "Oft-Shifted Foster Child Sues." As I prepare the final notes on this chapter, a news report appears which is worthy of citation. A sixteen-year-old boy, Dennis

Smith, has filed suit in Alameda County Superior Court, asking damages of $500,000 from the county social service agency and officials of the public school system there. In sixteen years he has lived in sixteen foster homes. "It's like a scar on your brain," he says. "I want people to realize what is happening to foster children." If he wins the suit, says Dennis, he will use most of the money to lobby for legislation to overhaul the foster parent system. In response to a question Dennis says that if adoptive parents offered him a home he would say no. "Because of what I've been through, I think I would take it out on them and I don't think it would be fair," he said.

6. DeCourcy, P., and DeCourcy, J. (1973): *A Silent Tragedy*. New York: Alfred Publishing Company.

7. Goldstein, J., Freud, A., and Solnit, A. (1973): *Beyond the Best Interests of the Child*. New York: The Free Press.

## Chapter IV

For "day care as it is," see Mary Keyserling, *Windows on Day Care*. For day care "at its best," see Sally Provence, Audrey Naylor, and June Patterson, *The Challenge of Daycare*. For a digest of information on employment of mothers and child care facilities, see *America's Children 1976*. Budget arithmetic is my own, worked out with consultation of experts.

1. All figures on day-care needs from Senate Finance Committee Child Care Data and Materials 1974, cited in *America's Children 1976* (1976). Washington: The National Council of Organizations for Children and Youth.

2. Provence, Sally, Naylor, Audrey, and Patterson, June (1977): *The Challenge of Daycare*, New Haven: Yale University Press, describes one such "ideal" center.

3. Keyserling, Mary D. (1972): *Windows on Day Care*. New York: National Council of Jewish Women.

4. Keyserling, Mary D. (1972): "The Magnitude of Day Care Need," in Van Loon, E. (ed.), *Inequality*

*in Education 13,* Cambridge: Center for Law and Education, Harvard University, pp. 5–55.

5. "When everyone is taking care of their own children, none of this important activity is counted in GNP. When everyone is taking care of each other's children, it is all counted. This accounting convention makes it appear as if something new, different and better is going on when, in fact, the opposite might very well be the case." Harold Shapiro (personal communication).

"If American society recognized home making and child rearing as productive work to be included in the national economic accounts (as is the case in at least one other nation) the receipt of welfare might not imply dependency. But we don't. It may be hoped the women's movement of the present time will change this. But as of the time I write it had not." Moynihan, Daniel P. (1972): *The Politics of a Guaranteed Income.* New York: Vintage Books, p. 17.

6. For summaries and analyses of the WIN program, see Moynihan, Daniel P. (1972): *The Politics of a Guaranteed Income,* New York: Vintage Books, and Levitan, Sar, Rein, M., and Marwick, D. (1972): *Work and Welfare Go Together,* Baltimore: The Johns Hopkins University Press.

## Chapter V

1. *America's Children 1976* (1976). Washington: The National Council of Organizations for Children and Youth, p. 32.

2. Ibid., p. 24.

3. Levitan, S., Rein, M., and Marwick, D. (1972): *Work and Welfare Go Together,* Baltimore: The Johns Hopkins University Press, p. 80.

4. Moynihan, D. P. (1972): *The Politics of a Guaranteed Income.* New York: Vintage Books, pp. 88–89.

5. Levitan, pp. 49–50.

6. Moynihan, pp. 29, 35–39, 85.

7. Ibid., p. 8.